HOW TO WRITE BOOKS THAT SELL

HOW TO WRITE BOOKS THAT SELL

Second Edition

BY
L. PERRY WILBUR
AND JON SAMSEL

ALLWORTH PRESS
NEW YORK

04   03   02   01   00   99   98   5   4   3   2   1

Published by Allworth Press
An imprint of Allworth Communications
10 East 23rd Street, New York, NY 10010

Cover design by Douglas Design Associates, New York, NY

Page composition/typography by SR Desktop Services, Ridge, NY

ISBN: 1-58115-006-7

Library of Congress Catalog Card Number: 98-72757

Printed in Canada

Contents

Interviews Help Breathe Life into Your Ideas
How to Be Ready for Every Interview
The Benefits of Research

When It's Time to Start the Writing
Finding the Right Place and Time to Write
The First Page Is the Hardest
The Importance of a Strong Introduction
Promise Yourself Little Rewards
Chapters Make Your Book
Advance Planning Pays Off
Chapter Headings Stimulate Your Writing
Vary the Lengths of Your Chapters
Some Chapters Are Tougher Than Others
Chapter One Sets the Theme of Your Book
Make Your Last Chapter as Good as the First
What About Length?
The Push to the Finish
Rewriting Makes a Good Book Great
Collaborations and Ghostwriting

Chapter Outlines Grab Attention
An Outline Can Build Enthusiasm
Elements of a Book Proposal
Length of Your Proposal
A Well-Written Book Proposal Serves as a Business Proposition
Why Many Authors Dislike Proposals and Outlines

How to Find the Right Publisher
How to Evaluate a Publishing Company
The Submission Process
Queries and Cover Letters
Hit Them with an Idea First
Good Idea, Wrong Publisher
Slush-Pile Submissions
How to Follow Up: Phone, Fax, E-mail, or Snail Mail?
How to Negotiate a Writing Deal
The Book Publishing Contract
Author Income: Advances, Royalties, and Ancillary Rights

Foreword

Lyndon Johnson does not rank high on my list of favorite presidents, but he did offer an occasional insight. This was his summary of political campaigns: "If you can remember to do *everything*, you'll win." Meaning that politics, like many pursuits, is a game of numbers where every vote might matter.

The same advice applies well to business, and make no mistake about it: Writing and marketing your book *is* a business. True, we writers are always telling ourselves, and anyone else who'll listen, that the artistry, the process of writing, and the personal growth we achieve is what really matters to us. Sure it is. I, too, am guilty of such self-deception, but it's just you and me here, so for once, let's be honest: What we really want is to be published, read, and admired by as many people as possible, and paid huge money to boot.

There, I've said it.

Toward the end of this book, L. Perry Wilbur and Jon Samsel relate how I marketed my first novel, *The Truth Machine*, a futuristic story about the race to develop a foolproof lie detector and what happens once it's unleashed on the world. Perry and Jon were also kind enough to leave *out* a few details. I would be remiss, however, if I failed to admit to the improbable stroke of luck that catapulted my first novel to public attention.

After I wrote the first draft of *The Truth Machine*, I collated dozens of copies of the manuscript and sent them to everyone I knew, begging for their feedback and suggestions. ("I take criticism really well," my cover letters assured them.) Then, aside from hiring editors to coach me, taking a night course in fiction writing, and reading every book and article I could get my hands on about writing and editing, I seriously considered thousands of often painfully insightful suggestions from friends and acquaintances. And, over an eight-month period, I rewrote *The Truth Machine* twenty-three times!

Obviously, the rewrites helped the novel a lot, so that was not the lucky part.

I had been unable to find an agent for *The Truth Machine*. In fact, like most first-time novelists, I couldn't even get an agent to read the book. Thus, I was forced to self-publish. I ordered books, hired a distributor, and, to raise awareness, I also posted the entire text free on the Internet for any reader willing to fill out a survey every ten chapters or so. The site became an immediate word-of-mouth hit, drawing over 15,000 visitors and 10,000 surveys in just three-and-a-half months.

But a few weeks after my books arrived from the printer, I received a call from Ballantine, the largest division of Random House, offering to buy out my distributor's contract, purchase my books (to rejacket and give away as promotion copies), pay me a six-figure advance, and republish my novel as their lead fall title amidst a cyclone of advertising and publicity.

Was this because they'd seen how well my book was selling in stores? Not likely. The books had barely arrived in stores when I received the call—way too soon to tell. Was it because of my Internet marketing? Nope. Ballantine was completely unaware of it. And once I told them, they didn't care at all.

In fact, they had read my novel only because a friend of mine, to whom I'd sent a manuscript and who happens to write coin books for them, had, unbeknownst to me, forwarded a copy to his Ballantine editor, suggesting he read it. Had I submitted *The Truth Machine* myself, it would either have been returned with a form letter explaining that they had no time to read unagented manuscripts, or it would have landed at the bottom of some editor's slush pile. But, instead, by the time Ballantine called me, every editor and vice president there had read—and loved—my book.

Dumb luck, as a result of doing . . . everything I could think of.

The harder and smarter you work and the more things you try, the more votes you'll get and the more likely you are to win. Not that I'm complaining, because all's well that ends well.

I think the book you're about to read, had it been available back when I was writing my first novel, could have improved my odds considerably. I recommend that you use it as a checklist, then try to add a few new ideas of your own.

I wish you great success.   —JAMES L. HALPERIN

James L. Halperin is the author of three novels and one work of nonfiction. His first book, *The Truth Machine*, is now a science-fiction cult classic. *The First Immortal*, published in 1998, is being produced as a CBS/Hallmark miniseries. His third novel, *Beginner's Luck*, is now being edited for publication. When he's not writing books, Halperin tends to his company, Heritage Rare Coin Galleries, the world's largest and most successful numismatic company.

Preface

The book you now hold in your hands is meant to help you write books and do it well. It's also meant to show you how to sell your books. Above all, this book will prove to you that you can finish manuscripts of your own. Writing a book is a marvelous adventure, and the only way to find out if you have the spirit for it is to take the plunge and do the book. Does the idea of bringing something new into the world appeal to you? If so, then you should gain real satisfaction from writing.

John Berendt was a magazine editor in New York when he decided to answer the call of his adventurous spirit. He went to Savannah, Georgia, with a tape recorder, walked the shady squares of that charming city, soaked up some of the town's flavor and atmosphere, and got to know its people. The result was a legal saga involving a killing, *Midnight in the Garden of Good and Evil*. Not too shabby for a book deemed "of limited regional interest" by certain publishers. Book publishers make mistakes and sometimes big whoppers. Never forget this truth as long as you write.

Darryl Wimberley, an unpublished author toiling away at his craft in Austin, Texas, could not arouse interest among agents or editors for any of his five completed novels. He decided he could not wait around for his career to "happen," so he hired a woman to submit ten manuscripts at a time to agents and, selectively, to editors at a limited number of publishing houses. The woman he hired sent him a clipping advertising a writing contest. Darryl's novels did not fit into any of the book categories the contest called for, but he figured, "What the heck, if I submit a manuscript, maybe it will spark the interest of one of the readers." Darryl submitted a manuscript and a few weeks later he received a telephone call from one of the contest organizers. His novel was *not* one of the semifinalists. But one of the readers loved Darryl's work and asked the contest organizers if they would put him in touch with the author. Two weeks later, Darryl had a two-book deal with St. Martin's Press.

The late Jim Fixx wrote what he knew. He was a daily jogger and well able to write a first-rate book on the subject. He thought his book would sell 30,000 copies. It did far better. It brought him $1 million in royalties in only fifteen months. But Fixx was lucky. His book came out just as the national jogging craze was hitting full force. The timing was great, and Jim's book quickly became a blockbuster success.

This anything-can-happen feature of the book business generates an excitement and a gusto, a feeling of potential that gives it a romantic aspect. There is a sense of satisfaction in being a part of such an industry. Despite being turned down, often by leading publishers, some books go on to become great successes and carve their own special places in the marketplace. Agents and editors may give certain books the heave-ho, only to see them still make it to the bestseller lists. The real lesson for every author is that no one agent's or editor's rejection should ever be taken as the final word.

We have tried to impart an energy, a dynamic spirit, into this book—to show not only the potential for today's author, but also the changing nature of the industry. The book was written for authors of nonfiction and fiction, but it should also be of help and interest to students of writing and journalism; to teachers of writing for use in courses, seminars, and conferences; to booksellers, reviewers, self-publishers, editors, and agents; to people in the business world; and anyone else interested in the world of books.

Many changes are taking place in today's book publishing industry, and authors need to be aware of them. The conglomerate invasion is having an impact on today's methods of producing, marketing, and promoting books. A special feature of the book is the specific guidance given on writing and selling all the major types of books including mass-market originals, romances, general-interest titles, business and professional books, children's books, how-tos, textbooks, scientific/technical works, computer books, and humorous books. There are also special chapters on writing and selling novels, the wide range of non-fiction book ideas, finding material for potential bestsellers, testing a book idea before it's developed, the truth about writing a bestseller, the crucial importance of book promotion today, self-publishing, electronic books, the Internet as a sales and promotional tool, and finding the right publisher or agent.

Scattered through the book is advice from, information about, and a look at the working methods of bestselling authors like Clive Cussler, John Grisham, Tom Clancy, Barbara Taylor Bradford, Neal Stephenson, Danielle Steel, Garrison Keillor, Jean Auel, Stephen King, Mary Higgins Clark, Arthur Hailey, James Michener, Ernest Hemingway, Barbara Cartland, Charles Dickens, and others.

Whatever your interest in, or connection with, the book business may be, this book is meant to guide and inform, instruct, entertain, and, above all, inspire you. It will hopefully make you wonder at the workings of the book business and, if you have never participated in the great adventure of creating a book for publication, enthuse you enough to try your hand at writing one or more books.

In the words of writer and book enthusiast David Dortorf, "Nothing is as lonely as the empty page. But the divine spirit moves us to fill it. . . . We writers are custodians of a proud heritage. We are the bearers of the divine spirit. We must write and write whether it sells or not . . . or is proclaimed unpublished. Writers and authors keep the divine spirit alive. To dare to be creative is to keep the world in something of a state of grace."

Aristotle put it this way: "The ennobling of the human spirit comes to us via the written word." Novelist Thomas Wolfe referred to the publishing process as "the naked, blazing power of print."

Let your heart and mind and spirit feed on this truth: Nobody in the book business really knows for sure what books will sell and what will capture the public's fancy and interest. Nobody knows what books will become the great success stories of tomorrow. That is one fact alone that makes the book publishing industry continuously fascinating year after year.

In spite of the conglomerates, mergers, takeovers, cancellations of author contracts (it happens), downsizing, cutbacks, letting editors go or firing them, the worship of the bottom line, and the breathless race for the next megabook, the majority of those who write books—part- or full-time—are happy people who would not change their lifestyles for anything. The truth is that most authors are not happy unless they are working on new projects. The more writing a real author does, the more he or she wants to do.

Even if you can devote just a few hours a week, or on weekends, to working on a book, we promise that your life will be enriched by the effort. And who knows? You may fall in love with the unique act of bringing a new book into existence and knowing that readers will be entertained, informed, or helped because of it. To hold a new book in your hand, nonfiction or novel, and know it's your baby, that you created it, is one of life's singular joys.

Acknowledgments

We would like to extend our gratitude to all our friends and associates who have contributed so much to making this book a reality. Many thanks to James Halperin, Neal Stephenson, Mary Kennan, Clive Cussler, Margot Maley, Tad Crawford, and the entire staff at Allworth Press.

My sincere thanks to my parents Barbara and Lyon Wilbur, and my brother Jack Wilbur, for their years of encouragement and interest in my writing.

—L.P.

I am blessed and forever grateful to have the following people in my life: My parents, John and Joan Samsel, who provided me with a secure childhood and always encouraged me to do great things—I love you. My sisters Joelle and Jeanine, who lent tender words of support when I needed them. My high school sweetheart Esther, whom I will love and cherish 'till death do us part. And finally, my heartfelt love to my daughter Cheyenne Claire, who provides the most endearing distractions from work possible. I love you more than you know.

—J.S.

The Book Publishing Industry Today: A Road Map for Writers

If Book Publishing 101 were a college course, most writers would be failing the class. And that's completely understandable. Writers are taught all their lives how to write—how to hone their craft and put their best efforts on paper. They may acquire related skills along the way, such as editing, rewriting, interviewing, researching, proposal writing, and even illustration, but each of these skills revolves around the central task they love—writing.

Book publishing in today's tangled landscape is a tricky business because more and more of the traditional "publisher duties," such as publicity and promotion, fall on the shoulders of the writer. Over the past ten years, the industry has evolved from a "you write it, we publish it" mentality, to a well planned and strategically executable co-production partnership. Writers who do not do their homework in *advance* of pursuing a book deal—researching their competition, creating a basic marketing and sales plan, developing a self-promotional campaign, drafting a killer proposal—have a much tougher time landing a publishing deal than their colleagues who do so.

Realities of Today's Publishing Industry

The author working alone happily, or with difficulty, sweating out a manuscript to completion: this is the heart of the book business. In my view, it always has been and always will be. But there are some grim realities that today's author should be aware of and try to keep in mind.

It takes more than an adventurous spirit and writing talent—as helpful and important as they both can be—to prevail in the publishing industry. Authors also need a thick skin and strong determination to succeed. Consider these facts:

- Conglomerates have soured the business to varying degrees (depending on who you are talking to). Certainly, many veteran publishing professionals, with years of experience, feel "the big boys, the corporate giants," have invaded publishing, bought and merged, and brought in their lineup of vice presidents, lawyers, and M.B.A.'s, all with one concern—the bottom line. This fact alone has changed publishing drastically from what it was in the good old days, which was a gentleman's business.

- As recently reported in the *Wall Street Journal*, "large super bookstores are mainly responsible for the book industry's current trouble."

- Online book wars are helping to drive down book prices (and profits), pitting Amazon.com (the king of online bookstores) against formidable foes such as barnesandnoble.com, Borders.com, and Books Now. The good news about online superstores is that they create more exposure for authors, which helps drive more sales for book products. The bad news is that there are less royalty dollars (per book) finding their way into author pockets.

- Books are being looked at more and more as products rather than as works of art. This means that humanists (writers and artists) need to invest some time and effort getting to know the book business and learning how to better promote their products.

- The growth of the Internet means that more information is available to consumers now than ever before, and authors need to compete for readers like any other media enterprise. Editors, authors, and publishers who understand this basic fact can position themselves to become the preferred information resource for tomorrow's digital consumer.

There is a rapidly growing amount of retail space available, but sales are not always keeping up with it. Adult hardcover sales have been falling in recent years, while money from adult paperback sales has grown by only a small percentage. The result is that publishers are bearing the burden and cost of filling this continuously increasing retail space, but are not receiving much benefit from it.

Today's book publishing industry is a moneymaking machine fueled by large media conglomerates caught up in the quest to boost stock prices by publishing as many blockbuster titles as the market will bear. One only need look at the book publishing industry's sister industry—the Hollywood film business—to notice similar patterns in business behavior. In Hollywood, it is almost impossible to predict which movies will generate hundreds and which movies will generate millions of dollars in revenue. Yet, hundreds of producers, writers, directors, and actors make deals and devote their time and effort to projects they hope will be some of the few to "make it." It's the lottery mentality (with only slightly better odds).

Likewise, it is hard to predict which book titles will sell in the hundreds and which will sell in the millions. Who would have thought that *Chicken Soup for the Soul*, an offbeat title published by a small press, would outsell all the O. J. Simpson murder trial books combined and launch a multimillion-dollar For the Soul book franchise?

"The conglomerate invasion has altered the book publishing business," claims Margot Maley, a successful book agent with San Diego–based Waterside Productions. "It benefits the big players—the John Grishams, the Stephen Kings, and the Michael Crichtons—but it hurts the mid- and backlist books. There is less money for advances on mid- and backlist books, and they get much less attention from the publishers. In the computer book industry there has been a recent wave of mergers. It has increased competition but hasn't necessarily affected the size of advances yet. MIS Press was just acquired by IDG, Van Nostrand Reinhold's computer division was sold to Wiley, and Ventana Press was folded into the Coriolis Group. These mergers may have come about because publishers have flooded the market with too many computer books in the past few years."

What's Considered a Hit?

The public is fickle, trends and issues change with the breeze, market forces skew business forecasts, you name it. Two key facts are known, however. A self-published title that sells over 15,000 units may be deemed a success. A small- to medium-sized press may need a title to sell 40,000–60,000 units to be considered a success. A large publishing house may need to sell 75,000 units or more to be labeled a hit title—and that's assuming the publisher did not pay the author a large advance against royalties.

But these are hit numbers. Many books never reach such bestseller status and, instead, enjoy a long life of moderate, consistent sales. Every author wants to write a hit title. But for every one title that "goes platinum," there are hundreds of other books that are making small profits or simply breaking even—and these authors are tickled to death that their books made it to market in the first place.

What's considered a hit to one author may not be considered a hit to another. What most authors do share is the desire to produce the best books they possibly can. And it's that singular goal that keeps the book publishing industry marching down the right path.

What Does This Mean for the Writer?

Consolidation in the book publishing industry is causing significant transformations in the way the bookstores, editors, publishers, and distributors function day to day. It may not be the best news for some, but it's not necessarily bad news for authors.

Many writers feel that the book market is more open than ever to new ideas. And the growth of the Internet has opened up regional book markets to a worldwide audience. That's exciting! The Internet has also spurred new revenue streams—such as licensing electronic versions of books, then distributing them to buyers over the Web. The Internet has also empowered writers to promote their books without having to leave their home offices, co-author books with writers thousands of miles away, communicate with editors and agents at the click of a mouse, conduct research in milliseconds, and order books with a credit card and a modem.

Change can be scary. And as an industry, the book world is in the midst of a tumultuous ride. Five hundred–odd years since the dawn of the printing press, we are now spiraling to the end of this grand millennium with wide eyes and great expectations. Don't blink. Your career as a successful book author demands your rapt attention.

CHAPTER 2

—————⊰•⊱—————

What Agents Really
Do for a Living

Author James Halperin published his first book without the benefit of an agent. His speculative novel, *The Truth Machine*, was forwarded to executives at Ballantine Books by another author. Amazingly, the book was rushed to press eight weeks after its discovery and became Ballantine's lead fall title. Noted author Judith Guest published her first novel without the services of an agent. *Ordinary People* went on to enjoy enormous success. Frankly, it puzzles me why people are often amazed when an author sells a book without an agent. It happens every day.

Agents are not gods with magic wands. They are not experts beyond reproach. In fact, I've heard it described this way: an "ex" is a has-been and a "spurt" is a drip under pressure! The truth of the matter is that a book project worthy of being published can be placed by yourself with some persistence and confidence. If it's not up to par, no one—not you or a top-notch agent—will be able to sell it.

Publishers Weekly once reported on an author who tried three different agents. Not one of them got her a book contract or even a magazine article sale. One agent lost some of her articles and demanded a 10 percent royalty on a book the author sold herself. Her reaction to this unhappy experience is worth remembering: "You shouldn't try to get an agent. There isn't a 10 percent difference between what you can get and what an agent can get for you."

Many writers, however, would disagree with this assessment. Some writers with little confidence in agents have handled the contract and rights details for their books themselves and have done well at it. Others, no doubt, have come out on the short end of the stick.

However, many authors have profited considerably from the services of a reliable and competent agent. The right one can be a real help to you, but the wrong one can actually hurt your chances for success. When you reach the point in your writing that you feel the need for an agent, you should weigh both sides of the question before arriving at a decision.

A Day in the Life of a Literary Agent

Here is how Margot Maley, an agent with Waterside Productions, Inc., the largest literary agency focusing on computer books, describes a typical day:

> There is no typical day in the life of a literary agent. But if I had to describe one, it would go something like this:
>
> I get to work about 8:45 and immediately get a large vat of coffee. I download my e-mail and check my messages and try to start answering e-mail before the phone starts ringing. Some days I'm on the phone nonstop from the moment I sit down until the time I leave. I could be negotiating deals or spending a good part of my day rescuing a book that's in trouble. Between phone calls I try to answer my e-mail. Unless I have a lunch meeting, I grab lunch somewhere quickly and bring it back to my desk. I try in the afternoons to send out my submissions and, if I have time, review the proposals and query letters that come in. I usually leave about 5:30 or 6:00 (unless I'm swamped), then I go to the gym, go home, and fall into bed.

What a Literary Agent Does for You

Agents serve a variety of functions—from selling an idea to schmooz-ing a deal. I've heard some longtime agents describe their job as part salesman, part counselor, part business manager, and part attorney. Whatever their function, the benefits of having an agent are numer-ous. According to Maley:

> An agent can serve a critical role in building a writer's career. We have contacts in the industry that the author most likely doesn't have. Most publishers will look at a proposal that comes from an agency more closely because they know it is targeted specifically for their publishing list. We know all of the ins and outs of each publishing contract and are able to point out red flags to our authors. We can also, with some degree of certainty, let them know what is and what is not negotiable.
>
> Lawyers, of course, can be used for contract negotiation, but if the lawyer doesn't have knowledge of the publishing industry, they can waste an inordinate amount of time negotiating clauses that don't have much bearing.
>
> We are always on the lookout for upcoming projects that might be a good fit for our authors. We are continually trying to develop our authors' careers in the direction they want it to go, and we don't encourage an author to sign a book deal simply because it's available.
>
> A big part of my job is troubleshooting problems that come up after the contract has been signed, helping writers deal with tight deadlines, and finding them help when their books are in trouble.

Generally, an agent's primary motivation is money. If an agent can get your books published with a minimal amount of effort and keep you working, he'll make 10 percent of your salary. Some agents insist that money is secondary to promoting your books and your writing style. Such agents believe that their primary function is to build careers for their writing clients, in the belief that they will be reward-ed for their efforts later on.

But beware. One prominent Hollywood literary agent (who will remain unnamed at his request) stated, "I don't build careers. I sign writers at their peak and ride them all the way into the dirt."

Whichever viewpoint you subscribe to, it is without doubt an advantage to have a literary agent represent your work. Here's why:

- A strong agent can often get a larger advance than you could get dealing directly with an editor. But this isn't always true and depends on a number of factors, such as your name value (if any), previous successes, and the type of book project.

- A good agent can be of great help with negotiating foreign rights. Many agents have branch offices or representatives overseas to handle such business. An alert publisher, however, can often take care of foreign rights for you. It can mean extra money for him, too, so he is not likely to overlook or mishandle this source of extra revenue.

- An agent relieves the author of business details. This means that a writer can focus on writing, without worrying about details. But for this very reason you'd better have a trusting relationship with your agent. Donald MacCampbell, who was a successful New York agent, advises authors in his book *The Writing Business* to personally meet an agent before signing up as a client: "You must try to meet an agent in person before you become involved, so that together you can assess the likelihood of a long-term relationship. It is very much the same as entering a marriage: you do not have to be in love, but you had better be damn good friends."

- If you intend to publish a number of books in the years ahead, the services of an agent are practically a must. You could lose a lot of money trying to handle everything yourself. However, if you plan only a few books, you could probably handle things yourself. In any case, most agents won't take on new clients until they've attained some success.

- Agents can sometimes show an author how to rewrite a project or book outline so that it will be accepted instead of rejected.

- If your books are mostly novels, the better agents are equipped to negotiate the film rights for you on any sales to Hollywood, and so are the publishers. Most of them have representatives on the West Coast.

- The author-agent relationship can grow into a lasting friendship. An agent shouldn't be expected to be a nursemaid to authors, but it helps to know that you are not alone, and that an agent cares and is pulling for you.

- Some agents allow their clients to call them to discuss various problems. Scott Meredith, another successful New York agent, truly liked his authors. He gave his home telephone number to each new client and took calls from some of his authors in the middle of the night. Like Donald MacCampbell, Meredith was also an author; he started writing at age fourteen. Something notable about MacCampbell and Meredith is that both had solid reputations for responding promptly to authors; some agents may take weeks or months.

- A respected agent can often get faster decisions on book proposals and outlines, as well as faster readings on complete manuscripts. Some agents claim they can get an initial reaction within forty-eight hours and a decision for an author within days, depending on the nature of the book. Unless you have a successful track record, dealing directly with editors may take months to over a year. An agent can save you a lot of time. And remember: time is the most valuable commodity a writer has. According to agent Ann Elmo, "A submission by an agent gets faster action by an editor. As to a reply from an editor, the proposal takes less time, of course—about a week or ten days."

- A good agent can be a vital link in matching the right author with the right editor. And authors with powerful agents representing them are not kept waiting long for responses. Most editors would not think of offending the powerhouse agents they deal with for fear of losing future contacts and submissions from those agents.

- In addition to books, some agents will also sell other material written by an author, including articles, motion picture screenplays, television scripts, and other literary properties. They know all the legal aspects, too, such as copyright and libel, that will help keep you out of trouble.

Other Benefits of an Agent

Still other sensible reasons for working with an agent (the right one) include:

- Your agent can encourage you when things aren't going well.

- Your agent can explain confusing clauses in a book contract and sometimes get you a better deal on subsidiary rights.

- An agent may well become a friend and someone you can bounce new ideas off of from time to time.

- Your agent can see to it that you get the best possible royalty rate, whether for a hardcover or paperback. Most leading publishers today are coordinating their companies to be able to publish and sell in all formats, hardcover and softcover, and even audiocassette.

Disadvantages of an Agent

You should also be aware that there are disadvantages to using an agent. These include:

- An agent takes 10–15 percent of your advances and royalties from book sales, and as much as 20 percent from foreign sales. Some writers prefer to keep all the money. In order to do this, the authors act as their own agents.

- Many writers, if not most of them, live outside New York City. Being "in the hinterlands" makes some of them feel isolated and concerned that an agent might favor in-town, on-the-spot authors. This is also true for writers overseas who live outside London, Paris, and the world's other literary centers.

- Some agents fail to communicate promptly with authors. Consequently, authors should not expect replies from agents within days or immediate action on all matters. An agent may have fifty, one hundred, or five hundred other clients. But an author deserves some initial reply regarding a project within six to eight weeks, even if it's only an acknowledgment that the material arrived safely. The better agents reply much faster.

- It is difficult for an out-of-town author to know who the most reliable agents are. It is easy to obtain a standard list of agents, but what's the story on each? Who are the most ethical agents? Some writers with one or more bad experiences with agents become suspicious and are cautious about signing with a new agent.

- Some agents charge reading or consideration fees, which many authors resent.

- Shocking as it may seem, some agents conveniently forget to send authors what is due them when it's time to settle up on royalties earned. Some unscrupulous agents have been known to keep money collected from overseas sales. They just fail to report the sales to the author.

- Using an agent for all contact with publishers prevents an author from gaining the experience of dealing with book editors directly. Many editors are courteous and reliable professionals with a keen interest in new books and ideas. An author can develop into a skilled salesperson by communicating with editors from time to time. In fact, some authors get so good at selling their books that they're advised on occasion to become agents themselves.

- The author's work may be handled by a minor employee who has little or no experience and/or clout in dealing with publishers. This can happen with the larger agencies.

- A smart writer can build his or her own list of good editors to contact. And if free to negotiate, such writers can communicate with the new publishers entering the business all the time. In other words, an author can sell at his or her own pace and level instead of the agent's.

- An author can choose to "auction" a book project to a number of selected publishers and then accept the best offer received (when the agent may not believe that an auction is appropriate for a particular project).

How to Get a Good Agent to Represent You

In general, you should seek an agent no later than after signing your second book contract. Many pros in publishing feel that a writer should find an agent after the very first sale. There's no guarantee that you will get a good agent after three or even five book sales. Some of the leading agents already have more clients than they can properly handle. Some won't even reply to letters from new authors or will send form rejection replies.

Get one bestseller on your credit list, however, and most agents worth their salt will come after you like bears that just spotted honey. A hot author naturally has a wider choice of agents.

Most authors simply write the agent (or agents) of their choice and explain how long they've been writing, list any published credits, book sales (if any), and other background information. They write about their work in progress and offer to send a synopsis, or outline, along with several chapters. In the case of a novel, they may have to send half or more of the manuscript. If the agent at the top of their list turns them down, they write to another one—and so on.

After trying the better agents for years without success, many writers give up and simply continue to represent themselves. Many of them do well on their own and later wonder why they spent so much time and effort seeking an agent. Others feel throughout their writing careers that they would have done much better if only they had been represented by a heavyweight (one with clout) New York agent.

The three best ways to land an agent in your corner are:

1. As discussed above, write directly to the agent and ask if he or she will consider your book.

2. Travel to New York City, Chicago, or Los Angeles (or wherever your agent is located), but write to the agent first and request an appointment. You must be able to convince the agent (in your letter) that seeing you will be worth his or her time. If you have a very commercial property to show, describe it just enough to arouse interest and curiosity.

3. Pick up the telephone and call the agent's office. Tell whoever answers the phone who you are, where you are calling from,

and why. Some lucky authors have gotten very good agents this way. They either called at the right moment or the agent simply happened to be accepting new clients at the time.

A Four-Star Way to Get an Agent

One smart way to snag an agent is to sell a book project yourself, then dangle the deal in front of the agent of your choice. This method often works, because it offers the agent tempting bait. In return for his attention and acceptance of you as a client, you drop a book sale in his lap and thus 10 percent (or whatever his commission is) of the advance and royalties the resulting book earns. Many agents find it hard to turn down such a sure thing. It's money in the bank for them.

TEN TIPS FOR WRITERS LOOKING TO GET PUBLISHED
(Courtesy of Margot Maley)

1. Research your market and competition.
2. Write a professional query letter.
3. Try to have realistic expectations. If you are Jay Leno and are writing about the talk-show industry, you can expect a huge advance. If you are trying to sell *One Hundred Funny Things That Cats Do*, don't expect millions.
4. Be willing to put in the effort to write a good proposal.
5. Be flexible.
6. Don't call every five minutes—professional writers are effective communicators.
7. Don't underestimate the amount of work it takes to write a book.
8. Don't miss your deadlines.
9. Don't undermine your career by bothering the publisher. Let your agent handle business issues directly with the publisher.
10. Try to write about something in which you are genuinely interested.

Some Final Realities About Agents

Agents have the real power in today's publishing industry. To a large degree, agents control what gets published. It's sad that editors have generally lost the considerable power they once had in the industry. They sit in meeting after meeting, read mostly agent submissions, and respond accordingly. Is it any wonder they have no time to reply or respond to unknown authors who dare to communicate from the hinterlands, take their precious time, or call them on the telephone (a real no-no with many editors)? It's almost enough to make Max Perkins and other great editors of the past come back to haunt them and the entire industry. Perkins, among others, respected all authors, treated them fairly, and responded to them promptly.

Remember, the large and powerful agents want to represent only those authors who have already "arrived" and are VIP names. Some writers have gone to New York to talk to agents and have returned discouraged because the better agents wouldn't take them on: their published credits weren't "important enough." If or when this happens to you, keep in mind that no agent really knows where the next big blockbuster book is coming from. Once you have given an agent a chance and are turned down, cross him off your list and contact another one. Or simply continue to represent yourself while learning everything about the business that you can.

Some so-called professional New York agents are incredibly rude to authors who contact them about possible representation. One wonders how some of these people ever sell a book to an editor. There is never any excuse for outright rudeness. The best way to retaliate is to write a bestseller. There are plenty of nice, courteous, and professional agents. So, if or when you run into a rude one, quickly move on to another. There are bound to be some bad apples in every barrel.

It is also true that agents face more pressures in this business. Like editors, they don't seem to have enough time to handle all their clients, see editors, pitch proposals, negotiate contracts, hold auctions (in some cases), and attend to the rest of their daily functions.

Peter Skolnik, a New York agent, says, "In the beginning of a publishing career, very often writers are in the position of being terribly

CHAPTER 3

Editors

In today's strange publishing era, an author should understand that the editor's role has changed. Instead of the line editing they used to do, many editors now spend most of their time in meetings, acquiring books, and dealing and communicating with agents. Even at smaller publishing houses, where editors may have more time to work closely with an author on his or her manuscript, the editor's role is not what it used to be.

While many authors prefer to think that most editors are professionals who care about them, this is not always the case. Just as with some authors, there are *some* prima donna editors convinced they are gods and thus should only have to deal with meganame authors and handle blockbuster books.

The day of the Max Perkins type of editor is gone. It was a different world when Perkins worked in his Fifth Avenue office. Perkins empathized with the plight of the novice book author. Now it's a publishing world of conglomerates, star editors, megastar authors, tremendous pressures, the bottom line, and the daily push and grind to snag the next blockbuster coming down the turnpike before another editor gets it. As a result, the lesser known, nonstar, nongod authors are often relegated to an author slush pile; meaning, if said editor gets the time to look at something, he or she will. If not, tough luck!

When you do find a responsive, professional editor to work with, do everything in your power to work harmoniously and effectively with that person. The author-editor relationship can be a very rewarding and happy one that can lead to more new books being published.

A Day in the Life of an Editor

Editors in major publishing houses never have enough time to accomplish everything, or so it seems to them. Their day is filled with an endless round of phone calls from "in the stable" authors, appointments with agents, acquisition duties, seeing current books they are handling through the publishing process, sales and marketing meetings, and more. Little wonder they have so little time for line editing.

Each book they shepherd through their house has its own set of details, possible problems, and related duties. The thing bugging most editors is the fact that there are simply too many books constantly coming through the pipeline. With 60,000 and more new books hitting the stores each year, imagine how overcrowded and cramped these editorial shepherds of the flocks must feel on many a day. Because of this, it's understandable why they have little time for lesser known or unknown authors from wherever.

Who knows? Even Max Perkins might have dropped a few notches in quality if he was given the pressures and time crunch most editors face today. Across the board, editors are beginning to receive a little more pay for their work, but they are still underpaid in many cases. The better, higher quality editors remain in the business, despite the low pay, because of their love of books.

It's interesting to note that one key editor was recently quoted as saying that some publishing executives have started "guessing" what books will sell big rather than relying on editorial judgment.

Regardless, and whether this is a trend or not, editors will never be replaced—especially the best ones with a true regard for good books and the authors who write them.

What Editors Do to Command Respect

From the viewpoint of many authors, simply replying and communicating with an author promptly wins respect. This is especially true for editors at major houses in New York, London, Toronto, Paris, and other key publishing centers.

Many authors agree that the longer it takes to get a response to a query, partial manuscript, or outline chapters, the higher the odds the response, if any, will be negative. If an editor likes a given project, the response is usually prompt. And if a powerful agent is involved, an author may get a report within days. In truth, some hotshot New York agents boast they can sometimes get decisions within twenty-four to forty-eight hours. Editors used to let authors know the status of a project (when some time had elapsed), but today they just don't have the time.

What else do editors do to command respect? The ones with vision, who are able to see the potential of a given book—whether nonfiction or fiction—will sometimes make very helpful suggestions for changes: a different chapter format, a new slant, or whatever.

Make no mistake about the fact that editors make mistakes. L. P. Wilbur once sat in a Doubleday editor's office discussing a proposed partial novel. The editor said, in a polite way, that the idea, the material, even the title, were "outside the Doubleday ballpark." Imagine the surprise of this author to see, a year later, the exact same title and idea in a published novel (albeit by another publisher), in the stores. Coincidences do happen. Needless to say, the author was still surprised.

Those editors who still see themselves as advocates for the books in their houses are usually very professional. In other words, the editors who get an author's book through the publishing process, and do it smoothly and on time, are valued and respected by authors.

Agent Margot Maley says, "Today's editors are working with tighter budgets but are expected to sign known authors, make sure the books are on time (critical in the computer book industry), juggle a million projects at once, and ensure that all of their advances earn out."

There are all kinds of details and schedules that editors must handle and coordinate in order to get a book through the system with no snags and in a timely fashion. One event that can torpedo this process and possibly kill a book before its birth is if the editor who is championing it moves to another publishing house. This scenario can spell disaster for the book because the advocate for it, the one guiding it through the system, is gone, and often no one else at the publishing house will care about the book like the absent editor did. When this unhappy event happens, the author rightly feels his or her book was a "stillborn" death.

When a book needs revision, an editor can offer advice and direction for an author, but given the hectic schedule of many editors, this guidance may be limited to certain or special authors whose books are the lead titles for a given season.

Author Neal Stephenson explains: "The role of an editor today is very complicated. It's partly to edit the manuscript and partly to act as the business manager or project manager for the book. It's damn near impossible to find someone committed to being a literary editor, who has the time, skill, and personality to sell the work. A lot of politicking and maneuvering is needed to get a book noticed in the marketplace. In the best of worlds, those two jobs would be separated. But they are not."

Editors who believe in authors and their books are highly valued and appreciated. James Michener often stated how helpful his editor was on various books, as his work usually needed to be heavily edited.

"When I first started writing, my manuscripts needed a lot of editing," recalls Stephenson. "By my third novel, I came to understand what the editor was doing and what kinds of things constituted 'bad writing' versus 'good writing.' I also calmed down a little bit. When I was younger, my big worry was that I wouldn't be able to write anything as long as a book. So I just wrote and wrote and wrote. My books were always too long and had to have tons of crap edited out. Later on, I realized that cranking out that many words is not that hard."

A number of the newer and younger editors are voicing and implementing new ideas about the ways books are acquired and sold. Some of these editors are promotion-minded, but they also include realistic editors who understand such issues as the rise of chain bookstores, escalating profit goals, the conglomerate takeover and consolidation, multimedia books, rising Internet sales, and the bottom line. A number of these younger and talented editors already command respect from authors for their prescient understanding of the new marketplace.

In truth, modern editors do a lot to command respect. Older authors who have been around awhile in the business sometimes remark that they remember the great power and prestige editors generally used to have. It is sad for these authors to see how many fine editors today are forced to play second fiddle and kowtow to powerful agents—jumping when they call or stop by, and "going through the hoops" so as not to offend them.

What an Author Should Look for in a Good Editor

The following tips for evaluating a good editor were provided by Brian Gill, a literary agent specializing in computer books for Studio B Productions, Inc. (*www.studiob.com*):

- You trust the editor enough to be honest with him or her.
- A good editor will return your phone calls typically within twenty-four hours.
- You'll find that you can work well with the editor who pushes you to create the best book possible. This may include some conflict, but it's conflict that creates a better book.
- The good editor will take some time to help you understand the publishing process and what will happen to your book at the publishing house.
- A good editor usually has been in the trenches for some time.
- Make sure your editor isn't working on five books (with similar deadlines) at the same time. It would be almost impossible for an editor to give you solid, quality feedback while trying to do the same for other authors.

A Final Word About Editors

To a surprising degree, editors have lost much of the power they once yielded. Their role as the gatekeepers of what gets published has been taken over by powerhouse agents who call the shots and exercise unbelievable control over the industry. Some of these high-clout agents will make it very clear, especially to newcomer authors, that their time and attention are reserved for meganame, blockbuster authors— "literary icons who have arrived and already made it."

Perhaps it will all change some day, but for the foreseeable future, certainly well into the twenty-first century, the power agents rule. God help those new or veteran authors without an agent in their corner, mediocre or with clout. You will likely endure some degree of abuse without an agent today. But like Howard Roark, in the great novel *The Fountainhead*, "the creative artist must be willing to sacrifice and endure for the sake of their work. It is the creative work, itself, that becomes the reward." When you hold your new book in your hands, and know that you gave it life, that you brought it into the world, you will know that whatever you had to face, endure, or sacrifice, it was worth it.

———◆◆◆———

What Kind of Book Do You Want to Write?

A key decision every author must make is what type of book to write. Should it be nonfiction or a novel? It is possible to alternate, providing you are skilled in both fiction and nonfiction, but you will most likely lean toward one or the other.

In the world of nonfiction books, there are self-help titles, business, how-to, humor, religious, scientific/technical, professional, mass-market originals, and more. Even in fiction there are subgenres like the romance novel and mass-market paperback. Many authors eventually find a single category in which they wish to specialize. The aim of this chapter is to help you decide where to focus your writing efforts by describing some of the more important categories in which books are being published.

The Self-Help Book

One of the most popular nonfiction categories is the self-help book. The range covered is wide, from a "teach yourself" series on a variety of subjects to books on achieving more success, money, skills, and a happier lifestyle.

Millions of readers out there want help of all kinds. Life may have them uptight in one way or another, or maybe they just haven't found the help they expected from magazines, newspapers, television, doctors, lawyers, parents, ministers, the government, or other sources. The help they are seeking may be in a book on how to raise their children, how to guide them through the dangerous teen years, or how to foot the bill for their children's college education. Maybe they want to lose weight, find a better doctor, plan a more exciting vacation, learn a new skill, develop a hobby, insulate their home, prevent a heart attack, or plan and give a speech. There are a lot more potential subjects for a self-help book. The point of this type of book is that it offers practical help to the reader and provides specific information.

How to Know If You're Really in Love is a how-to title; but it's also a self-help book. Some titles bridge both categories. *When Work Doesn't Work Anymore: Women, Work, and Identity* was a lead nonfiction title for Delacorte. It's a good example of a self-help book. Some self-help authors build impressive lists of published titles, and a glance at leading mail-order publications shows that self-help books are selling well. Like other categories, sales of this type of book can go through cycles—peaking at times, yet falling off at others. One thing is certain: the companies selling such books would not continue to run expensive ads for them if sales were not good. Many self-help books are profitable for their authors, and books in this category can stay in print for years.

Why You Might Try a Self-Help Book

A case can be made for writing almost any kind of book. To help you decide if this is the right category for you, ask yourself the following questions:

- Do you have a real interest in one or more self-help subjects?

- Do you have special knowledge, training, or experience in some area that can be applied to a self-help book?

- Do you enjoy helping others or like the idea that a book you write might help at least a number of readers?

- Do you have access to the information needed for a book of this kind?
- Does the research needed for a book offering self-help seem interesting to you?
- Have you developed a plan that has proven of some help to you, and do you believe others could profit from it?

Even if none of these questions seems to strike a chord with you, it does not mean that the self-help book is outside your ballpark. They are meant to be a list of clues to consider as a potential self-help author. One or more of these questions may stimulate you to look at the same subject as everybody else and think of something different—resulting in a book that might just make a difference in somebody's life.

The Thriller: A Book for All Seasons

The thriller is another popular category, but in the world of fiction. Perhaps the first step, before considering this category, is to find out if you can write fiction.

Author Mary Higgins Clark is a master of the suspense thriller. In *Pretend You Don't See Her*, a young woman is in the wrong place at the wrong time and gets caught up in a murder investigation. The variety found in the thriller category is fresh and appealing. *Gatekeeper* by Philip Shelby is a harrowing tale of murder and deception where heroine Hollis Fremont finds herself in the middle of a plot to assassinate the leading candidate for presidency of the United States. The candidate is being stalked by someone called the Handyman, who is also after Fremont because she seems to have something the assassin needs.

As you might expect from this high-tech world in which we live, an increasing number of thrillers involve computers. Stephen Cannell's *Final Victim* is about a serial killer who uses secret computer technology to trap his victims. In recent years, the legal thriller has been very popular as both novel and motion picture. *The Rainmaker*, *Runaway Jury*, and *Street Lawyer*, by John Grisham, have done well. And another exciting thriller is Michael Crichton's *Airframe*, which poses the question of why a plane on its way to America from the Far

East goes through a series of sharp up-and-down movements just before crashing.

Asking intriguing questions is a key way to launch a thriller. What if Dr. Jekyll had a maidservant? This question led to *Mary Reilly*, by Valerie Martin, which became a motion picture with Julia Roberts in the lead. What if a young lawyer wished to be a photographer, and after killing his wife's lover (who was one), assumes the identity and vocation of the victim? This premise by Douglas Kennedy, an Australian author, became *The Big Picture*.

A novelist's own life may yield good ideas for a thriller. Tap your memory for story ideas. The places you have been, scenes you have observed, even bits of conversation can all lead to a novel. Interesting people you have met, seen, or know about, from all walks of life, might lead to the beginning of a thriller. Think about your own life, your past, as well as what happens each day.

Keep in mind that a number of thriller novels go on to become very successful blockbusters. Whether you're a new author or veteran pro interested in breaking into the thriller category, stay alert to the fact that publishing has become more and more like Hollywood. Both publishers and the film industry are looking for big, mega-blockbuster properties. Turn one of these out and place it with the right publisher, with or without an agent (it's tougher to do this without an agent), and you could skyrocket as an author.

Books for Children

With some writing experience and knowledge behind you, you might one day wish to try your hand at a children's book. Books for children are special and take special talents. You need a keen understanding of the children of this generation.

How does an author get started writing for children? Maurice Sendak, Theodor Geisel (Dr. Seuss), and Judy Blume probably wondered the same thing when they began. The way Blume started was to write the kind of realistic books that appealed to her as a child: "Realizing I would never be another Dr. Seuss or Maurice Sendak, I turned to novels and wrote the kind of books I wanted to read when I was a kid."

An understanding of today's children is vital for success. Children do not like to be talked down to, and they are not easily fooled. The more you know about them, the better your chances of writing a successful book.

When you feel ready to try a project, query a likely children's book publisher with a description of your idea or an outline and chapter or two. Some publishers require a complete manuscript. If you are not sure which publishers to contact, look over the special announcements of new children's books found in *Publishers Weekly, Poet and Author, Writer's Digest,* and other trade publications. Study the newest books for children and see which publishers seem to be doing the type of book you wish to write.

Some publishers break down their juvenile and children's book needs into these divisions:

- Picture books for children ages three to eight or four through seven.

- Fiction and nonfiction for ages eight through twelve. Readers from eight to twelve often enjoy books about faraway places.

- Humorous novels and science fiction for ages nine through twelve.

- Special-interest books for young to older teens eleven through eighteen. Young teens like books on careers, hobbies, the family, government, problems young people face, and romance. The older teen group is more into special interest areas like military service, art, music, and theater.

Many children's book authors started young. P. L. Travers, author of the Mary Poppins books, started writing as a girl. Her early stories and poems were published in Australian magazines and newspapers. While recovering from a serious illness, Travers wrote the first few Mary Poppins stories "to while away the days, but also to put down something that had been in my mind for a long time." Travers is very loyal to her young readers. She calls them "children hopping about with umbrellas, trying to make them fly."

An interesting recent development in children's books is the entrance into the American market of two new British publishers. This, of course, has been done before and very successfully. The reaction to this move falls into two camps: some believe there is room for two more; others feel it will simply add to an already overcrowded field.

The focus of one of these companies, Element Children's Books, is spirituality for kids. This focus developed from conversations with children, teachers, and librarians. "Teachers and librarians commented that there was nothing written on such subjects as body-mind-spirit specifically for children." Element decided it was time to fill this need. Element will publish about forty books a year. They will be edited and produced in England and published on both sides of the Atlantic.

The other publisher entering the American market is Barefoot Books, which has previously done picture books, story anthologies, and collections of fairy tales. New books planned by Barefoot include *Forest Tales from Far and Wide*, *A Fairytale from Old Russia*, and *Tales of Wisdom and Wonder*.

Writing the Young Adult Book

Some very successful books in this field have been *Anastasia Has the Answers*, *Find a Stranger*, and *Say Good-Bye*. Their author, Lois Lowry, has stated that the most important thing in writing for a young audience is, "If I'm asked to remember when I was ten, I feel being ten—I see it, but I can also smell it and taste it. For me, that's the most important thing in writing for kids."

Young adult books are frequently sold with audio tapes. Evidently, parents agree with publishers that combining young adult books with tapes is sensible, practical, and beneficial. Parents who use these book/tape packages derive a feeling that they're teaching their children themselves. It certainly also provides an engaging alternative to television.

By hearing the tape, young adults benefit from imagining what the characters in the story look like. Reading skills are improved too. Parents have caught on to these new benefits for their children, and this part of the industry—book/tape combinations—is an exciting phase of the industry.

Judy Blume has been one of the most successful and popular young adult authors. One of her books, *Are You There God? It's Me, Margaret*, is the story of a child's life. She has since done a string of very successful books, and her young adult readers eagerly await each of her new titles. Blume was once a teacher at New York University. She went through two years of rejections before publishers began to buy her books. She refused to give up. In a ten-year period, she wrote seven books. Today, her books bring her thousands of letters a year. Her specialty is writing about the secrets of children and their problems.

C. S. Lewis is another popular author who was successful as both a children's author and a philosopher/novelist. He explored the experience of reading in *An Experiment in Criticism*, and constructed a heartfelt fantasy in *The Chronicles of Narnia*. He also retold the mythical tale of Psyche and Cupid in *Till We Have Faces: A Myth Retold*, and wrote *C. S. Lewis Letters to Children* as well.

Young adult books can keep selling for years. Some have sold for twenty years and longer. This may motivate an author sooner or later to try writing one. And each new crop of young people means more potential readers. As Maurice Sendak has said, "We stay in print for decades."

You may find a happy and successful place as an author in this field. If so, you will be helping to shape the men and women of tomorrow. That is an exciting challenge. Children and young adults are special. And that goes double for the books written for them.

If you are interested in writing for this audience, you should check out the latest books for young adult readers to see what's working in today's marketplace. Some recent titles worth reading are:

Library Lil   *Seven Brave Women*
Animal Smarts   *The Surprise Family*
Buffalo Days   *Wolf Stalker*
Turtle Dreams   *The Science Book for Girls*
What Is the Full Moon Full of?   *Insects Are My Life*
As Long as There Are Mountains   *Daily Life in a Covered Wagon*
Marvin's Best Christmas Present Ever   *Where Did All the Dragons Go?*
Too Many Pumpkins   *Cat, You Better Come Home*
Alice Ramsey's Grand Adventure

The Textbook Market

There are writers who cringe at the very thought of doing a textbook. "All that technical and detailed work would get on my nerves," they say. Or, "I would rather write mass-market paperbacks, children's books, or general nonfiction trade books."

Textbooks are definitely worth the time and effort necessary to write and sell them—or, rather, sell and write them. (Remember, the smart author sells first and then completes the manuscript.) More and more large-sized paperbacks are being used in the classroom, and textbooks don't have to be dry accumulations of technical and complicated details. In fact, the accent now is on texts that communicate in less technical and more engaging ways.

Consider this. Just one successful textbook used by the junior college market can bring $40,000 a year or more for its author. This is assuming that the book sells for at least a respectable price. Many such books retail at $50 or $65, and even close to $100. Some lucky authors with good textbook sales call them "golden annuities."

The trick to hitting it big with textbooks is to write one that is adopted by community colleges, regular four-year universities, and other schools. Textbooks that catch on can be used for many years. If they do become bibles in their respective subject areas, their authors make a lot of money.

One highly acclaimed author wrote a math textbook that was widely used. He has reportedly realized well over a million dollars so far from this one book.

WHAT TEACHERS WANT

According to *Instructor* magazine, the majority of the lower-grade teachers believe there should be more emphasis on reading and writing skills. A new focus on these skills will improve student achievement, in their opinion. Of 8,500 teachers polled, just over 41 percent strongly agreed on the need for better textbooks.

Educators need and want better textbooks. If you can write a better quality textbook that does the job more effectively than existing textbooks and that students will find engaging, you might well have a winner. According to some critics, "American textbooks read as if they were written by neutrals in the struggle between freedom and slavery." One publishing executive, Marlowe Teig, countered with this reply: "I think careful examination of the entire texts would reveal that, in fact, U.S. textbook publishers and their authors are far more negative and critical of some countries than some examples would suggest."

In *Why Are They Lying to Our Children?*, author Herbert London claims that children's textbooks have a number of statements in them that are "misguided, misleading, or wrong." According to London, examples of such statements in children's textbooks include the following myths:

- The world population has been doubling every thirty-five years.

- The greenhouse effect will melt the polar ice caps, thus destroying civilization.

- Sixteen percent of the world's people go to bed hungry each night.

- Since 1954, Americans have used more minerals than the rest of the world has used since the beginning of human history.

- Every new demand on our environment may cause the collapse of our ecological system.

London's book makes the case that mankind is not only better off than ever, but that worldwide progress will continue to improve the life of the average person. The crucial point for our discussion, however, is the need to be very accurate in any textbook you write. That means knowing the subject and being up-to-date with current research. If or when the book is adopted and used in the schools, thousands of students may be influenced and affected by your textbook. It is worth all the effort to make it accurate and truthful.

THE MARKETPLACE

Royalties for textbooks often range from 8 to 15 percent of the net price received by the publisher. Because schools and colleges order at bulk prices, authors' royalties are based on the net revenue received by a publisher for a specific textbook. Royalties are smaller for an elementary or high school textbook. Some authors with a good track record, however, may obtain higher royalty rates. There have been reports of some textbook authors receiving a 20 percent royalty.

Top markets for textbooks are elementary schools, high schools, junior colleges, community colleges, four-year universities, university extension programs, graduate schools, trade schools, and continuing adult education. Depending on your expertise, you may be able to write a textbook for any of these areas.

If you have done any teaching, you should find it easier to complete a textbook. A teacher or professor already knows a great deal about his or her subject, which could be brought to the writing of a textbook. Teaching experience is a definite advantage. Another way to find a possible textbook subject is to take strong interests or hobbies that might be marketable to one of the areas listed above. If you are an accomplished woodworker, for example, you may be able to write a textbook on the subject that would find a market in elementary and high schools, junior and community colleges, trade schools, or continuing education programs.

The best time to sell a textbook is early. Make an outline of what the book would cover, and try to interest a suitable textbook publisher. Given today's publishing arena, it is to your benefit to write several chapters of your textbook to include with your proposal. But start seeking publishers before wading too far into writing the whole book. Even if they're interested in your proposal, publishers often have their own ideas that they'll want included in the book. Textbooks are usually longer than general trade books, often running at least four hundred or five hundred pages. A positive change in the textbook business is the increased harmony between store managers and publishers. There is a much more professional relationship between colleges and publishers than in previous years.

Is writing a textbook for you? The only way to find out is to try your hand at it. Explore possible subjects; perhaps talk to college professors and teachers about their textbook needs, and visit college bookstores to see the books currently being used by students.

Some authors discover that they like this category so much they decide to specialize in it. It is quite an achievement to see your own textbook published and to know that it is used in colleges or schools and that students are learning from it.

New Age and Religious Books

People in and out of the publishing industry have predicted a fading of interest in New Age books, but so far it has not happened. In fact, the New Age sections of many bookstores have grown. Religious books also continue to sell well as people everywhere try to cope with their problems.

New Age books appeal to all ages and address the mind-body-spirit, occult, psychic powers, ESP, angels, near-death experiences, and other subjects. Some bookstores display New Age titles in interesting and creative ways, which adds to their attraction. The New Age category is fascinating to many authors and draws them like a magnet. Attending a mind-body-spirit or New Age conference is a good way to get an idea of how many readers are fans of this category and the vast array of books offered in it.

Stephen O'Brien's New Age books are classic examples of the genre. Stephen is one of England's busiest and most popular mediums. His books on life after death have sold well in many countries, and he is in demand as a speaker. His book *Angels by My Side* is a compelling and fascinating read.

One rapidly growing publisher of New Age (mind-body-spirit) books is Llewellyn of St. Paul, Minnesota. The company divides its line of books into the following categories:

ESP and the Paranormal	Numerology
Crystals	Palmistry
Dreams	Psychology
Astrology	Relationships and Romance
Health and Herbs	Religion
Magic	Tarot
Hypnosis and Programming	UFOs
Meditation	Women's Studies
Mythology	Yoga
Divination	Recovery and Self-Help
Creative Visualization	Spiritual Sciences
Ecology	Shamanism

Some of Llewellyn's titles include:

The Power of Dreaming
Summoning Spirits
How to Read the Tarot
The Healer's Manual
How to Heal with Color
Scottish Witchcraft
The Magic in Food
The Magician's Companion
Poltergeist: A Study in Destructive Haunting
The Truth about Psychic Powers
How to Uncover Your Past Lives

Religious and inspirational books have been selling briskly in recent years. These books may not be purely evangelical, but they often uplift the human spirit, provide light along life's way, and point to the eternal values of love, beauty, hope, and faith.

Strong proof that inspirational books can take off and sell big-time are such current titles as Dr. James C. Dobson's *Parenting Isn't For Cowards*, which has sold nearly 700,000 copies, and *Small Miracles*, which has sold 130,000 to date. There are times when religious books far outsell the widely reported bestsellers. The compilers of the various bestseller lists don't generally check with religious bookstores, and a number of top-selling religious books don't show up on such lists.

Most publishers now realize the importance of the religious market. A study conducted by Knowledge Industry Publications cited a trend that has had a favorable influence on sales of religious books, namely, the aging of the population.

More than thirty religious books have sold over a million copies within a five-year period. And today they continue to sell more. One book alone, *The Living Bible*, sold an incredible 18 million copies in five years. According to an editor at Doubleday, one of the fastest-selling books that company has ever published is *Angels: God's Secret Agents* by Billy Graham.

When and if you try your hand at this category, consider this: if your religious or inspirational book project is one that could cross borders and sell in both secular (general) and religious markets, try to place your book with a general publisher that includes religious/inspirational titles in its line because it will be in a better position to market the book to a wide general audience.

One reward of writing a religious/inspirational book is the satisfaction of knowing your book may have helped someone at a crucial time in their life. Another factor that can keep you enthused is the variety of subjects that can be treated within the category. Author Thomas Moore, for example, wrote about sex in *The Soul of Sex: Cultivating Life as an Act of Love*. He wrote about love in *The Education of the Heart* and he wrote about the soul in his book, *Soul Mates: Honoring the Mysteries of Love and Relationship*. Other rewards are the opportunity to explain what your own faith means to you, the chance to lead others closer to God, and the satisfaction of knowing your book may be around for years or decades to come.

If you are considering writing for this category, the following are some popular religious/inspirational books worth familiarizing yourself with:

Random Acts of Kindness
The Celestine Prophecy: An Adventure
Crossing the Threshold of Hope
Blessed Expectations
Spiritual Path
Prayers for Healing
Sacred Living
The Woman's Book of Spirit
In Touch with God
Illuminata
Talking to Heaven: A Medium's Message of Life after Death

Laugh Along with Humor Books

Legendary actor (now an icon) Humphrey Bogart once remarked that "the world is forty laughs behind." Laughter and humor are part and parcel of what makes life worth living. Life would be terribly grim without humor, and there lies the reason for the success of this type of book. To be able to laugh at yourself, at and with others, and to appreciate the humor in many of life's situations is to live more fully and intelligently.

Humor is many things. It's the wit and artful comedy often seen on the stage and screen. Humor is sarcasm, satire, the effective use of exaggeration, perhaps a play on words, a situation real or imagined that brings laughter, and much more. There is dry humor; slapstick; wit; a biting, sometimes painful or sharp humor; and even sick humor. There is country humor, political humor, business humor, military-service humor, prison humor, wedding-day humor, joke humor, single-punch-line humor, movie and television humor, car-decal humor, and so on down the line.

The Nothing Book was a mind-boggling success with more than a million copies sold. There was in fact nothing in the book between the covers but blank pages. The *Official Preppy Handbook* was a big-selling book in the eighties, and the same is true for certain books by contemporary comedians and humorists, including the works of Dave Barry, Drew Carey, P. J. O'Rourke, Jeff Foxworthy, Art Buchwald, the late Erma Bombeck, and other funny people with a knack for transferring their talent to book pages.

Humor book authors seem to either have it or not. Comedy writing is not easy. Otherwise, why would so many comedians use a lot of writers? You may be great as a stand-up comic, but can you get that humor to work on the written page?

If you are considering writing this type of book, do some serious thinking about what makes humor work, what lies behind it. Why do some people laugh so easily and others far less? Do certain kinds of humor fare better and, if so, why? It will help you to stay alert to the spontaneous humor that erupts in your daily life. A good place to start is by thinking about the bits of humor you might bring into the lives of your neighbors, friends, associates, spouse, family members, relatives, and others. Then try to actually do it. Share that humor with them. It's wonderful to bring a laugh or smile to anyone, and if you can bring it to the people around you, maybe you can bring it to the readers of a humor book.

Simplicity is often a key factor in the art of humor. English comic writer Thomas Hood summed it up well: "The sense of humor is the just balance of all the faculties of man, the best security against the price of knowledge and the conceits of the imagination, the strongest inducement to submit with a wise and pious patience to the vicissitudes of human existence."

So what about it? Is there a humor book in you? If you have a talent for making people laugh, you should certainly consider this type of book. If you are good with jokes, humorous stories, or even more idiosyncratic forms of humor, you might be able to transfer this ability to the page and finish a book in this category.

Some humor books worth examining are:

Babies and Other Hazards of Sex: How to Make a Tiny Person in Only Nine Months With Tools You Probably Have Around the Home

Byte Me!: Computing for the Terminally Frustrated!

Dirty Jokes and Beer: Stories of the Unrefined

Everything I Need to Know about Succeeding in Hollywood I Learned from My Pit-Bull

The Bachelor Home Companion: A Practical Guide to Keeping House Like a Pig

Politically Correct Bedtime Stories

Get Your Tongue out of My Mouth, I'm Kissing You Good-Bye

Six Degrees of Kevin Bacon

Guidelines for the Romance Novel

Publishers have finally seen the light when it comes to romance and women's fiction. They now realize that these are very often best-selling books. Ask the average reader (and many authors agree) about romance novels and the usual response is, "There's a glut of them, far too many." Yet, they continue to sell. The increase in electronic sales and book-club money has raised the stakes in this category. Book-club sales in this category reportedly rose 17 percent in 1996. As the Internet reaches more and more people, romance sales should rise— and quickly.

To begin with, too many people think of authors in this category as morons. They are entertainers, and the books they turn out offer entertainment value. For a lucky number of them, a great deal of money can be made in this category. If you want to specialize in romance novels, you must be persistent and keep your eye on the target constantly.

Romance novels always bring the reader a sense of fulfillment, hope, and a positive view of things. They usually have happy endings and offer readers pure escape from their humdrum lives. Women are obviously the big buyers of these books, and they want plenty of action and romance, and generous amounts of sex. Women authors often do incredibly well with even their first few books in this field. Part of the reason romance novels succeed is that they fill a desire for love and romance. A huge number of women all over the world never get enough of either in their lives.

These books transport their readers into exciting worlds of romance, passion, and often suspense. They allow their readers to forget their own troubles for a while and to share the glamour of the books' settings and the experiences of their heroines. Despite the apparent glut, romance novels are here to stay. If you enjoy reading romance novels, that may be a clue you should try this special category.

Some popular romance authors are LaVyrle Spencer, Janice Graham, Victoria Barrett, Amanda Ashley, Laura Abbot, Jill Jones, and there are many others. Here are some typical romance novels that are doing well:

Destiny's Warrior	*The Lady of the Lake*
Desire Me Only	*Nothing but Velvet*
Beside a Dreamswept Sea	*Silver Tomorrows*
The Black Sheep	*Mystic Memories*
His Cinderella Bride	*Looking for a Miracle*
Eternal Vows	*Ever His Bride*
Across the Rainbow	*Into the Morning*
Touch of Enchantment	*The Lady from Spain*
Shores of Desire	*Essence of My Desire*
Journey of the Heart	*Double Deception*
Silken Betrayal	*Lone Star Rancher*

To sell in this category, you must know what you're doing and really offer an entertaining book that sweeps the reader into another world, one that is glamorous, intriguing, and, above all, romantic.

The Barbara Cartland formula is to start with a very handsome duke, marquis, or other titled hero who is haunted by some dark family secret. He meets a virginal, penniless woman and they fall in love. A wicked relative is usually lurking around, and a lot of period detail continuously crops up in the story. Cartland sets most of her books in the late nineteenth century. She has often said that it has a "sweetness people crave today."

Today, the competition in the field of romance novels is so fierce that you simply *must* have a strong story and tell it well. New elements are also being added to the romance novel. One example is the time-travel romances that are now offered.

Romance novels account for over 50 percent of all mass-market fiction. The top names in this category turn out two to four new romances a year, and most of them love their work.

Here are some guidelines for writing a romance novel:

1. First, realize from the start that readers of this kind of book want escape. Make sure you provide it.
2. Your main character will often emerge from the era or background you have chosen to write about. As best you can, live the life of the heroine in your mind. Identify with her as the story progresses.
3. Make sure you have a strong theme for your romance before you begin. If you can express the theme to yourself in one simple sentence, so much the better.
4. Develop a difficult situation for your heroine to face. Remember, too, that the man in your heroine's life is a source of strength. He helps her to cope with a trying situation.
5. Pick a day to start on your romance novel, whether it's doing research, planning and writing an outline, or completing the first pages of the actual book.
6. Set a goal of so many pages a day or week or so many chapters over a certain time. Then work toward that goal.

Once you have about fifty pages and an outline, you can try to interest an agent or editor. Be sure to write first for an okay to send your material, rather than just mailing it in cold. If it's expected, it's more likely to get quicker attention and a faster reply.

7. Try to make the dialogue in your romance ring true. Ask yourself if it sounds right for the characters to say the lines and words you give them.

8. Read your manuscript critically and rewrite the parts that need it. Writing is rewriting; you will improve your book with each draft you write.

Finally, do not give up if one or a dozen publishers reject your romance. Publishers make mistakes, and some of the best books ever produced were turned down by companies many times. Never give up if you believe in your book.

The Wide Appeal of How-To Books

How-to books cover just about all areas of life today. Just name a subject, and chances are good there is a how-to book on it. The megabookseller Barnes and Noble estimates how-to books account for about 30 percent of trade sales. How-to books have wide appeal and often become strong sellers. Many become backlist titles and keep cranking out sales for publishers and royalties for their authors for years.

Jon Samsel co-authored the book you have in your hands plus four additional how-to books in eighteen months. He also wrote two business white papers and wrote/produced an interactive handbook for Apple Computer during that same time period. It's true, however, that some authors have a natural feel and strong ability for this particular type of book.

Here are some examples of how-to books on a range of subjects:

How to Build a Real Estate Money Machine

Writing for Interactive Media: The Complete Guide

How to Shoot Stock Photos That Sell

How to Start and Succeed as an Artist

How to Pitch and Promote Your Songs

Retire Smart

Your Living Trust and Estate Plan: How to Maximize Your Family's Assets and Protect Your Loved Ones

The Rigors of the Scientific/Technical Book

Scientific and technical books are growing in demand. Sales have been rising for a number of years, and the figures prove this growth is expected to continue. Sales in this area have usually doubled at least every seven to eight years.

This category includes books covering many disciplines and subjects, including space and astronomy, mathematics, nutrition, entomology, minerals, hazardous waste, robotics, genetics, aging, noise effects, birds, and anatomy. While there is a wide choice of subjects about which to write in the scientific/technical field, obviously the author should know the discipline or subject matter well. Scientists, doctors, and engineers are especially in demand by editors to write on their specialty. But they are often too busy with their work and may consider writing a book of lesser importance. Editors sometimes have a tough time convincing them to do a book.

That's why even if you are not a doctor, scientist, or engineer, you may still write a book in this field. But it goes without saying that you better have easy access to an expert before tackling a technical or scientific subject. You absolutely must know the discipline or subject extremely well for success with this sort of book.

This type of writing must be clear, accurate, concise, and reflect considerable knowledge. The scientific facts and all technical terms in such books must be correct. The explanations and terms involved are often complicated and hard to communicate in a simple way. They may lose the reader at any point if not done well.

Technical writers often have a background writing in one or more of the following forms:

- Technical or scientific papers
- Reports
- PowerPoint presentations (multimedia)

- Technical articles and special research studies
- Advertisements
- Abstracts
- White papers
- Technical oral presentations
- Proposals

Such experience is helpful since many scientific/technical books reflect years of intense study. In some cases, entire decades of research, study, and experiment have gone into the labor of a single book.

Why do the authors of such books—especially scientific experts with top credentials—decide to take on the projects? What are their motivating factors and influences? In a number of cases, the financial reward can be substantial. But even stronger influences include the chance to develop a new course, the possibility that students may use the book and benefit from it, and the sense of being able to contribute an outstanding text that may well become a leader in its field. Publishing the book offers a chance of prestige for the author. This is a very strong incentive.

If you are not an expert or authority on a given technical subject, don't rule out writing this type of book. You may become an authority on a particular discipline, or subject, in the future. Once you have had articles published on a subject in respected magazines and journals, you move closer to the ranks of being an authority on it. Your degree of knowledge and expertise increases with each new article you write. Papers, oral presentations, reports, and anything you learn and communicate about the subject lifts you higher on the authority ladder. At some point, you may consider yourself ready to write a book about the topic. You have paid your dues and have become a well-informed authority on the subject.

You should realize that any publishers you approach are going to ask for your credentials in the field. The more you can cite, the greater your chance of getting a publisher interested. Keep in mind that book ideas in this scientific/technical area may originate with an editor. Find out, if you can, what specific subjects may be of special interest to individual editors. This could start the ball rolling for you.

Business, Professional, and Computer Books

Business books are always in demand and are now likely to be located near the front, if not in the front sections, of most bookstores. A number of bookstores have special sections for books about investing, running a small business, careers, and management. Marketing and salesmanship books often have their own subdivision. Computer books are usually placed very close to the business section, so customers are led easily and naturally from the business to the computer section or vice versa.

Business books offer career strategies, ways of increasing productivity, tips on finding a job, advice on getting and doing well in interviews, marketing products, and starting one's own business. They offer real help and comfort, and a number of them become bestsellers. By the turn of the century, Americans alone will spend nearly a billion dollars a year on business-related books. Business books are so hot at this time that the category offers new authors one of the best ways to break into print.

Business experience is something many people can claim. If you come up with the killer idea for a book on sales, training and coaching, job skills, any number of management strategies, leadership, business philosophy, productivity and job performance, computer user manuals, or true stories of well-known businesspeople, you may land a publishing deal.

What is the reason for the spectacular rise of interest in business books? Simple. It's the desire for information. We are in an era often referred to as the information age. Knowing where to get the right information and how to use it is power. This demand for information is expected to continue in the twenty-first century. This enormous (and growing) customer base has fueled a book publishing frenzy. It includes books about how to access and manage information with high-tech tools like computers and the Internet.

Margot Maley represents writers in the computer field and claims that the top publishers in today's computer/technology industry are Macmillan, IDG, Microsoft Press, and O'Reilly. Maley explains that "they are all successful for different reasons":

Macmillan owns six different imprints and each imprint has a best-selling series. IDG had great success with their Dummies books and built on it. Their Bibles and Secrets books also sell very well. Microsoft Press has the advantage of inside information and access to an author base of very talented Microsoft employees. They are careful to publish high-quality books; they can't afford to have incorrect information out there. O'Reilly publishes high-quality books for which they see a strong need. They don't necessarily follow the crowd in terms of hot topics, but all of their books have a long shelf life and are famous among programmers as the best books out there.

As already mentioned, Maley's firm, Waterside Productions, is the largest literary agency focusing on computer books. "We sell an average of 350 books a year, of which about 90 percent are computer books," asserts Maley. "We have offices in San Diego, San Francisco, Hawaii, and just opened a New York office. For eight years now we have hosted the Waterside Publishing Conference in San Diego. The conference is aimed at authors and publishers in the computer book industry and has become quite famous to those in the field."

Some of Waterside's top clients include: Andy Rathbone, the author of *Windows for Dummies*; Peter Norton, who wrote *Inside the PC*; Alan Simpson, who wrote several bestselling Mastering books, including *Mastering WordPerfect*; Dan Gookin, the author of *DOS for Dummies* and father of the entire Dummies series; Danny Goodman, author of *The HyperCard Handbook*; Roger Parker, who wrote *Looking Good in Print*; Bill Simon, who just finished *On the Firing Line* with Gil Amelio (former Apple CEO); and Rick Smolan, who wrote the book and produced the CD-ROM for *Passage to Vietnam* and *Twenty-Four Hours in Cyberspace*.

One of Waterside's most successful book deals is *Windows for Dummies*. It has spawned a series that has become publishing legend. *Windows for Dummies* has also done extremely well, having sold well over four million copies so far. It was the first computer book ever put on the *New York Times* bestseller list. Waterside also represented Alexander Besher's techno–sci-fi novel *Rim*, which was optioned by TriStar Pictures and has been translated into fifteen languages.

The success of computer and technology books such as these has acted like a super tonic for the business category. The result is that business books, in all areas, are booming. Business books have become big business like never before. If you are considering writing a business or computer book, keep in mind that many popular business publishers like books that arrange their subject matter in attractive ways, thus drawing many extra readers to the works. This is not only a matter of book design but includes features introduced by the writer, such as a step-by-step format.

Expert testimony can also help boost a business book. Quotes by known authorities on the subject add credibility to the text. You can also use anecdotes or stories to drive a point home. These stories keep readers interested and offer variety. Charts, tables, the use of comparisons and contrast, definition of terms, and other helpful tools will all give your book more power and appeal.

Here, in a nutshell, are some of the better reasons for writing a business book:

- Business books sell better than other, more general categories.

- Many editors are interested in acquiring new business books. If yours gets turned down by a few editors, there are a number of others you can try.

- You may already have firsthand business knowledge that you could put to work in a book. You may, for example, know a lot about real estate, direct marketing, advertising, management, or investing.

- Foreign publishers are often interested in the rights to business books published in America, since the same information can benefit readers overseas.

- Business books can keep paying royalties for their authors for years and perhaps decades.

One top business book editor has stated that he believes business humor is a growth area in this field. Since most business books are serious, the need for, and appeal of, lighter humor books in this category is a natural development. Adrian Zackheim, publisher of HarperCollins's business division, believes that "people buy business books and personal finance out of a perceived need."

Business books worth investigating include:

The Motley Fool Investment Guide: How the Fool Beats Wall Street's Wise Men and How You Can Too

The Millionaire Next Door: The Surprising Secrets of America's Wealthy

Growing Up Digital: The Rise of the Net Generation

The Profit Zone: How Strategic Business Design Will Lead You to Tomorrow's Profits

Selling the Invisible: A Field Guide to Modern Marketing

Crossing the Chasm: Marketing and Selling High-Tech Products to Mainstream Customers

Swim with the Sharks without Being Eaten Alive

The Art of Leadership

Reinventing the Corporation

Dead Ahead: The Web Dilemma and the New Rules of Business

Blur: The Speed of Change in the Connected Economy

If this area interests you, here is a plan for how to sell a business book. First, make a list from business directories found in the larger libraries of the companies and corporations in your fields of interest and knowledge. Next, write the public relations director or president of each company you select. Give some background information about yourself and describe any special knowledge or experience you have in connection with that company's business. Ask if there is any interest in a book related to the company.

This is a way to interest a specific company in hiring you to write a book. It's possible that a corporation may buy a book you write for it outright, pay royalties, license your content and "re-brand" it as their own, or work out some other financial arrangement. The other way is to go the standard publisher route and offer a proposal or completed manuscript to a business publisher. Before you do, write to a number of publishers and request copies of their latest catalogs so you can study their lists of books.

The following directories can be helpful to you in your search for corporations:

National Directory of Associations
National Directory of Public Relations Directors
Public Relations Register
MacRae's Blue Book (Index of Companies)

You can also go online and use any of the major search engines such as Yahoo, Webcrawler, Hotbot, and Excite, or visit online directories such as Hoovers Online (*www.hoovers.com*), CorpTech (*www.corptech. com*), or CompaniesOnline (*www.companiesonline.com*), which will help you in your search for corporations with which to work.

One author, Virginia Hamilton, decided that having her own Web site was one way to generate business. She was hesitant at first, but now realizes a number of advantages: "The site is for people of all ages to know me and my work. I make personal connections to people all over the world."

You might consider having a Web site of your own. It would allow you, as an author, to communicate directly with editors, readers, parents, teachers, and others about the books you write and have on the market. A Web site is a very convenient way for business book buyers to become familiar with your work and can convey a professional, businesslike air that works to your advantage.

Mass-Market Paperback Originals

Some of the biggest money an author can ever hope to make lies in mass-market paperbacks. For example, one such volume, *When Bad Things Happen to Good People*, has over two million copies in print. Only time and experimentation will tell if you have what it takes to turn out this type of book. Paperbacks cover a wide variety of subjects.

How do you know if your idea is right for this category? There is a test you can do. First, ask yourself if enough people would be interested in the book. "Mass market" means it must appeal to millions of readers. Then ask if your book is commercial enough for the leading paperback publishers (remember, what they want is huge megabook blockbusters). They do, however, make some big mistakes in the books they reject and then watch them soar to the heights.

Finally, in your test, ask yourself if you have enough interest in the idea to see it through to completion. Writing can be hard work. You would be surprised how many manuscripts are started but never finished.

Bestselling author Clive Cussler started in mass market with his *Raise the Titanic* years ago, but it was suddenly right on target with the smash success of the new *Titanic* film that soared to $1 billion in worldwide receipts. Most of Cussler's books are now released in hardcover, but he has sold millions of paperbacks as well. In a three-book deal, before he even started writing, he was reportedly offered $14 million. But Cussler made it to the big time some years ago and has long been a well-known name in fiction. He is one of the nicest, most modest, and professional authors in the business.

The lead character in his exciting novels is Dirk Pitt, who gets involved in challenging missions on the high seas of world intrigue. The first thing you realize about Cussler is what a truly masterful storyteller he is. For novels, that is the most important skill you can have. Cussler simply tells a fascinating story—as reading his novels reveals.

When not working on a new novel, Cussler and his crew are usually off to some distant locale on a search for a new sunken ship. He is credited with having located the German U-boat that sank the *Lusitania*. They located the exact spot where the U-boat lies beneath the sea and passed along that information to officials for the historical record.

In writing novels, Cussler believes that a novelist should make every effort to end each chapter with a hook, so the reader feels, My God, what happens next? This is what keeps readers turning pages.

Keep in mind that mass-market paperbacks can be nonfiction and not just novels. Consider the following mass-market paperback bestsellers:

Don't Sweat the Small Stuff . . . and It's All Small Stuff
Chicken Soup for the Woman's Soul
Spontaneous Healing
The Seven Habits of Highly Effective People
How the Irish Saved Civilization
All I Really Need to Know I Learned in Kindergarten

The first named, *Don't Sweat the Small Stuff,* is reportedly the fastest selling trade paperback ever. It has gone back to press many times for a present total of some 4.5 million copies sold.

If mass market interests you, the first thing you need to decide is whether to try writing a nonfiction book or novel. Study the best-seller charts to see what the public is responding to at present. Some books cross borders and sell in every area. This fact is presenting new challenges to publishers. But if writing for the mass market is your goal, think wide appeal. Put excitement, adventure, mystery, glamour, and suspense into your fiction. If your mass-market effort lies in non-fiction, strive to come up with news the reader can put to immediate use. Above all, try to anticipate coming trends and look for sequel books, which are simply other angles on the same title or idea.

Some major mass-market paperback publishers are:

Bantam
Avon
Warner
Penguin Putnam
Berkeley
Random House
HarperCollins
Ballantine
Dell
Fawcett
Vintage
Doubleday/Anchor

—❖—

What It Takes to Write a Novel

Robert Louis Stevenson was a hardworking novelist though a semi-invalid. While lying in bed during one illness, he started a new work and emerged with the full manuscript after writing nonstop for days. He read it to his wife, who criticized it.

Stevenson became enraged and threw the manuscript into the fire, saying his wife was right about it. He promptly returned to his bed with pencil and fresh paper. He wrote for three more days with little sleep and emerged again with a completely new manuscript of the same idea. The slender 149-page book, *The Strange Case of Dr. Jekyll and Mr. Hyde*, was published in 1886. When the *London Times* praised the new book, it quickly became a bestseller, selling 40,000 copies in six months.

Ah, the novel. *There* lies a challenge, whether it's the great American novel, Scottish, British, or whatever. How many people have vowed to write a novel and see it published? Lots. But just completing one, especially a worthy book, is a considerable achievement.

The world of published novels includes such memorable classics as *The Call of the Wild, The Time Machine, The Power and the Glory, The*

Catcher in the Rye, Fahrenheit 451, How Green Was My Valley, Great Expectations, War of the Worlds, The Great Gatsby, A Tale of Two Cities, This Side of Paradise, Gone with the Wind, David Copperfield, Little Women, Doctor Zhivago, What Makes Sammy Run? and contemporary works such as *Executive Orders, The Firm, Microserfs, A Dangerous Fortune, The Truth Machine, The First Wives Club, Neuromancer, Midnight in the Garden of Good and Evil,* and *Snow Crash.*

A Good Idea and the Desire to Develop It

Anyone can try to write a novel, but here are some essential up-front tips that will vastly improve your chances of completing one.

There is no guarantee that if you have a good idea for a novel that you're going to actually develop it. Many people have, no doubt, thought of strong story ideas but never got around to writing even the first word. A good idea coupled with the desire to develop it form a strong combination. If the desire to write is there and the idea keeps asking to be developed, this may be enough to get you started.

Prolific writer Jerry Pournelle has a good line that goes something like this: "In order to become a writer, all you have to do is write a million words and throw them away."

If you try to anticipate what people are going to like and try to write that way, you will drive yourself crazy. Publishers and agents can smell a book that was written to get published. That doesn't mean they won't publish it. Some books that were written to get published will make a lot of money.

According to author Neal Stephenson, "Writing is all about connecting with an audience. There is no recipe for doing that. If what you are writing is fiction, then all bets are off. There is no one way to come up with an idea for a novel that people are going to like. I wrote two novels that I thought people would like (*Zodiac: An Eco-thriller* and *The Diamond Age*) and they didn't do very well. Then I decided to write something completely weird and off the wall because I was pissed off. I just thought, *I'll show them.* I wrote *Snow Crash* and that's what got my career going."

First-time novelists often come up with all sorts of reasons why they shouldn't start work on a novel. The success of the venture depends on the author's determination. Charles Frazier's debut novel, *Cold Mountain*, was a National Book Award winner and one of only four novels to run over fifteen weeks on the bestseller charts. It stayed in first place for eleven weeks. The point is that a first novel may take off and become a blockbuster.

A major reason John Grisham's novels do so well is the fact that they are based on strong story ideas. His ninth novel, *The Street Lawyer*, is about an armed homeless man who takes nine attorneys hostage from a Washington, D.C. law firm. That is the scene with which Grisham opens his novel, and it rivets reader attention. Grisham followed his writing "hobby" in the 1980s and completed *A Time to Kill* in 1987. The very next day he started *The Firm*.

Ray Bradbury took some twenty years in the making of a murder mystery titled *Death Is a Lonely Business*. As Bradbury puts it, "I had to wait for the characters to come one at a time and ask to be in the book."

The bottom line is this: if the subject or idea for a novel is engrossing and gripping to the author, he or she will usually follow through and develop it in writing.

The Time and Freedom to Write

"If only I had the time and freedom to write, I'd turn out a hell of a novel!" That is the claim, or boast, of many a person. It is of course one thing to talk about writing a novel and something else to do it.

Having the time and freedom to write has made it possible for some people to complete their novels. George Sand left her home, husband, and children for Paris and the time and freedom to write. She cared little for her husband but missed her children terribly.

At first she arranged to spend six months of each year in Paris and the other six back at home; this freedom and time to write encouraged her to develop good work habits early. She had a goal of writing no less than twenty (some reports say thirty) pages each night.

Sand would not retire for the night until she had finished her regular stint with paper and pen. It was one of the reasons for her success and helped to make her an established author. Her amorous adventures, outspoken opinions, and daring (for that era) novels all combined to make George Sand the talk of Paris before she was thirty.

Abandoning home and family is not the only way to find time to write. Florida Fox News anchorman Bill O'Reilly evidently kept his job and still found time to complete his novel titled *Those Who Trespass: A Novel of Murder and Television.*

Many authors with little time and freedom still manage to turn out good work. They get up several hours early, before the rest of the workaday world has risen, and knock out a number of pages before going to a full-time job. Others work on their novels during the evenings after work, and on weekends. Even if an author must work at a daily job in an office, plant, school, or wherever, he or she can still find enough time and freedom in a week to move that new novel along.

James Webb, secretary of the Navy, has written three bestselling novels and now has a fourth one in the works, *The Emperor's General,* which reportedly brought him an advance somewhere between $500,000 and $1 million.

The Key Elements of a Good Novel

A good novel has five essentials, and without them the chances are less that your book will find a home. These five musts are conflict, character, dialogue, setting, and action. Be sure your novel has all five and you may have a chance. Let's take a look at each.

Conflict

What is a story, a novel, without conflict? The answer is, dull. Real life is saturated with conflict, and fiction needs it too. Think of the conflict in *Wuthering Heights, Gone with the Wind,* and other books. When Scarlett vowed she would "never be hungry again," she was rising victoriously above the struggle of bouncing back from the ravages of the Civil War and all it had done to her, her family, and her beloved Tara.

Character

In a sense, readers of novels enter the lives of fictional characters, and this is all the more reason to have an intriguing lead (major character) in a book. When you write fiction you are speaking *with* character and action, not *about* character and action.

What would Jane Eyre do next? That is what holds the readers' attention and keeps them turning the pages. Think of the female lawyer in John Grisham's *The Client*, the retired country scholar turned knight-errant in Miguel de Cervantes's *Don Quixote de la Mancha*, the copy boy turned studio mogul in Budd Schulberg's *What Makes Sammy Run?* the coal miner turned labor activist in Ken Follett's *A Place Called Freedom*, the condemned adulteress in Nathaniel Hawthorne's *The Scarlet Letter*, the lowly rebel against society in George Orwell's *1984*, the young hard-boiled detective in Dashiell Hammett's *The Maltese Falcon*, and other unforgettable characters. In every case, particularly the classic novels, there is a very strong character smack in the middle of conflict.

Dialogue

An exchange of words between characters is dialogue, and it is dialogue that reveals the ongoing story. Any novel without enough dialogue simply dies on the vine because there is not enough going on between the characters. Can you imagine *Oliver Twist* or *A Tale of Two Cities* with little or no dialogue?

Setting

Some authors believe the setting of a novel makes little difference. Others think it has an important bearing on the total result, keeping the author (and often the reader) interested. Hemingway set one of his short stories, "A Well-Lighted Place," in a favorite café he frequented. John Berendt's *Midnight in the Garden of Good and Evil* would not be the same book if the setting were anywhere else but Savannah. In fact, the book's popularity is due in part to the author's ability to breathe life into the setting.

Action

What happens, the pace of events in the unfolding story, is the action. If nothing much happens, there would be little action. Take the popular male hero action stories like the James Bond series and you have a good example of action in a novel. Daniel Silva's razor-sharp suspense novel, *The Mark of the Assassin*, takes the reader on an action-packed journey around the world. In Ken Follett's *The Pillars of the Earth*, readers are plunged into a brutal, twelfth-century struggle for the succession of the English throne.

An Intriguing Character

A character can be so vital that an author eventually feels compelled to give him or her life on paper. Nicholas Evans's *The Loop* spotlights a biologist and specialist in wolves, who travels to Montana to protect a wolf pack that has been causing trouble in a ranch town. *When the Wind Blows*, by James Patterson, is about two completely engaging characters. The novel focuses on protagonist Frannie O'Neill, a Colorado veterinarian who is recovering from the mysterious death of her husband, and on Max, a little girl born with wings, who is at the center of a massive conspiracy involving secret genetic research.

Many successful novelists go through an "incubation period"; they live with their characters a long while before getting them into a book. Because of this, they often write a stronger, more readable novel than they otherwise would have.

It's wise to introduce your main character in the very first paragraph of your novel, or as soon thereafter as possible. If you can, try also to present the situation, the kernel out of which the action will unfold, or at least part of it in the first few paragraphs. Every novel is a story of character, and character in fiction can be developed by action, reaction, explanation, effect, and speech. The story of a novel moves forward through the use of dialogue.

Clive Cussler created a most intriguing character in Dirk Pitt. His latest book starring Pitt, *Flood Tide*, has sold a whopping 600,000 copies and counting. Some tips from Cussler are very helpful and worth remembering:

- The ending is absolutely vital. "Readers want the good guys to win and the villains to lose."

- "A novelist is an inventor creating a product. If the product is not good, you aren't going to sell it."

- "If you're really a book writer, before you finish one book, you've got an idea for the next one."

- "I always send in the *finished* product (manuscript). I prefer to do it this way."

- "Try and resolve a problem in a book before you go on to another one."

- "I write one page at a time. The word processor is so nice. With the word processor, I edit a chapter on the screen till it's ready. I go back and change a few sentences and add something."

- "When I type the end, I'm usually through. I may go back and do a little rewriting."

- "A good editor or agent will read the first paragraph and if it doesn't take off, forget it."

- "I try to write a fast-paced book. The meat of the story is dialogue. The heavier the dialogue, the faster the pace."

- "When I'm working on a book, I never read."

- "An author should get an office and write all day. There are too many interruptions at home."

Clive Cussler goes out of his way to encourage authors and share his views about the business. He has been an inspiration to many authors. There is an old adage in publishing and writing in general that "writers/authors are insanely jealous of each other." In some cases, it is quite true. In the case of the talented Clive Cussler, you would never know what enormous success he has achieved in novel writing. Quite simply, he is one of the nicest people in the publishing business with a highly developed ability for writing adventure novels.

A Title, Theme, Mood, or Feeling

The sources of novel ideas are numerous. Even your own life can yield good ideas. Something you read in a book, magazine, or newspaper can set the wheels in motion.

Jack London was a sailor, adventurer, and gold prospector before he began to write, so he had a lot of real experiences to use in his work. His *John Barleycorn* is a powerful novel that deals with London's alcoholism. *The Call of the Wild* reveals his interest in animal heroes.

Joseph Finder's *The Zero Hour* is a thriller about a female FBI agent in pursuit of a terrorist hired to wreck Wall Street. Sheri Holman's debut novel, *A Stolen Tongue*, is about a religious pilgrimage embarked on by a Dominican friar. In Phyllis Alesia Perry's first novel, *Stigmata*, a young woman is troubled by ghosts from the past; they appear to her after she sleeps under an old quilt embroidered with scenes from her great-grandmother's life.

Sometimes all an author needs is an initial spark or idea association. A title might leap out from the printed page or come to you while you're walking the dog or taking a shower. A feeling you have on a rainy day, a sad, depressed, or happy mood, or even just a lone phrase may all suggest a possible novel.

Terror specialist Stephen King likes to place ordinary people in unusual situations. He writes to entertain himself, as well as the reader. "The main difference between going to the movies and writing scary books is that you pay to go to the movies. For writing, they pay you," says King.

According to Ray Bradbury, "All of the good, weird stories I've written are based on things I've dredged out of my subconscious. That's the real stuff. Everything else is fake."

As a young girl growing up in Atlanta, Margaret Mitchell heard many true stories about the Civil War. It was then natural that her novel idea was a story about the old South.

Novelist Paul Theroux taught in Singapore and Uganda and used these locations for his early novels.

The fading of drive-in movie theaters led one author to write *The Flamingo Rising*, which tells of a family that runs, and lives behind, the largest drive-in theater in America.

Concrete Observations

Details from life not only enrich novels, they often spark ideas for them. Mark Twain wrote about the emotions of people in rural settings and no doubt got many of his initial ideas through observation.

Stay alert daily to what is going on around you and in the world. Your observations could in turn lead to ideas for a novel.

L. P. Wilbur still remembers standing in Grand Central Station in New York City for the first time. Thousands of people were rushing past on all sides, and many had just arrived on trains. Others were hurrying to leave, buy a ticket, or meet someone else coming into the city. The thought struck: "Busy crossroads of a nation." What of the problems many of those people faced? What of their happiness, careers, challenges, hopes, dreams, and enthusiasm for life so evident on many of their faces? The line from an old radio show surfaced: "A thousand dramas played daily." That is what life is, only it's millions of dramas. That phrase effectively summed up the life in that busy station. Key phrases can sometimes provide the first spark that leads to a novel. The phrases above inspired Wilbur to write his novel *A Million Dramas*.

A man desperate to feed his wife and child steals a loaf of bread and is sentenced to twenty years. This simple idea became Victor Hugo's unforgettable *Les Misérables*.

Ideas for novels are all around you if you train your mind and heart and spirit to become aware of them.

Discipline

Many fine novels might have never been published if the authors had not been willing to pay the price in discipline. Some get up at four or five each morning to finish several new pages of a novel. While working on his novels, John O'Hara often wrote all night. The late James Michener spent years of work on his superb novels. He was well known for the pains he took in presenting the history of the locale through which he weaved his characters and story.

Authors also need the discipline not to give up if publishers say no to their novels, whether it's the first one or seventh. The faith an author has in his or her books may well be tested. Some top novels were rejected ten or twenty times, and by major publishers, before going on to become mega-bestsellers.

It doesn't stop there. Authors need discipline to promote their books once published. That means contacting radio and television talk shows to line up interviews, getting reviews, sparking articles in local and regional newspapers, getting the interest of book clubs, attending conferences, and bringing the book to the attention of media people who can generate publicity and interest in it.

Top-selling novelist Barbara Taylor Bradford explains: "There's only one reason to write a novel: that is because writing fiction is absolutely essential to one's well-being. In other words, it's the work that really counts, the sense of creation."

Ray Bradbury advises: "All you should worry about is whether you're doing it every day and whether you're having fun with it. If not, find the reason. You may be doing something you shouldn't be doing."

The sticky point is this: novels are composed of scenes, and it takes discipline to get those scenes right and believable. When each scene ends, the reader should know something more, and feel something more.

Danielle Steel describes her writing routine this way: "My books come to me in little pieces; first I get a kind of vision about it, then gradually, bit by bit, it all comes together. It takes me a good six months to get a full outline. I've literally finished a book and started another the same day." Think of the discipline it takes to spend six months on an outline.

F. Scott Fitzgerald said it this way: "To make the reader see is an author's main purpose." That requires the discipline to rewrite until you have it right. Fitzgerald also said this about the act of writing: "You must begin by making notes. You may have to make notes for years. Put an idea down when you think of it. You may never recapture it quite as vividly the second time."

Fitzgerald focused on emotion. "Whether it's something that happened twenty years ago or only yesterday, I must start out with an emotion—one that's close to me and that I can understand."

Think of the discipline of Ernest Hemingway in his early writing years. During those years he got pitifully small checks from little magazines. But he kept at it and eventually became one of the giants of modern literature.

The words of John Grisham are in order here as well: "The only pressure I put on myself is to write the best book I can write. I guess one of these days I'm going to publish a book and it's going to be a real dud that will sell half of what the last one sold. At that point, I'll probably worry about sales."

Advantages of Writing a Novel

Most professional novelists have their own list of advantages in writing novels. Some of the direct benefits of novel writing include the following:

- You gain experience in telling a story and in how to use fiction techniques, such as the flashback.

- You gain confidence in yourself because you actually prove you can do it.

- You learn firsthand how plot, dialogue, character, and conflict can all work together to produce an intriguing story.

- You find out what type of novel you can write best—especially if you experiment in different categories or genres.

- You are better able to compare novel writing with nonfiction so you can decide which you prefer.

- The up-front money authors receive for a novel (in the form of an advance against royalties) can often be much larger than the advance for a factual book. It depends on how enthused your publisher or agent is about your novel. This is also especially true when paperback publishers show interest in the reprint rights to hardcover novels. Keep in mind that the author's reputation and track record have an influence on the size of the advance.

- Novels have a better chance of being sold to film companies.

Types of Novels to Write

If novel writing is for you, then you have an interesting choice of book types from which to choose. Whether you are a new author or a seasoned veteran, looking over the various types of novels you might write can be helpful. Most of the main genres are included in the following:

- Adventure novels

- Suspense and thrillers

- Mysteries

- Romance novels

- Science-fiction novels

- Occult and supernatural novels

- Gothic novels

- Fantasy novels

- Horror novels

- Mainstream novels

- Historical novels

- Juvenile or young adult novels

The above is not a complete list, and some of those listed can be broken down into divisions. Chances are, however, that you will find the type of book you want to do among those named.

Examples of some top-selling novels include:

The Partner
The Third Twin
The Ranch
Jurassic Park
Pearl Moon
Empire of the Ants
Cat and Mouse
Plum Island
The Church of Dead Girls
Cold Mountain
Paradise
Memoirs of a Geisha
The Runaway Jury
Pandora
Black and Blue

Some major fiction publishers are:

Crown
Delacorte
Knopf
Ballantine
Doubleday
Little, Brown
Warner
Henry Holt
Atlantic Monthly Press
Random House

CHAPTER   6

———❦———

The Nonfiction Book

U nless your mind and heart are set on writing novels, the nonfiction book offers you a great deal of choice and potential. This chapter will make that case and may get you interested in this type of book. Keep in mind that a number of authors write both fiction and nonfiction.

To begin with—and this is a considerable incentive to focus on nonfiction—a book based in fact generally grabs a publisher's interest more easily than fiction. A main reason for this is the fact that a nonfiction book usually means less financial risk than a novel. Publishers believe in making sound business decisions and want to publish books that will earn back their investments and, hopefully, make a decent profit. They sometimes take a flier on a novel, but most publishers cannot do it too often. Their overall goal is to publish books that will earn money in the marketplace and turn in a good showing.

A nonfiction book will also save you time because it can often be sold to a publisher on the basis of an outline and several chapters or a proposal. For novels, quite a few publishers want to see the finished manuscript, or most of it, before making a decision. Take your pick. Wouldn't you rather sell a portion of a book than have to complete an entire manuscript on speculation?

It can take years for a novel to make the rounds of publishers before finding a home. During that time you could possibly sell several nonfiction books and finish writing them. These are realities that you must consider.

Author Neal Stephenson observes: "I think that there is a huge market for people who can explain complicated things well. If you look at the work of John McPhee, for example, there is a guy who can take a subject like oranges or mud slides that seems completely dry and dull, and write something about it that is fascinating. That's because he understands the subject and can write clearly. The world is full of strange and complicated things that people have a need to understand, but don't. It's not easy to write nonfiction, but there are huge opportunities to write in that field."

Your Automatic Credentials

A key advantage to writing a nonfiction book is that you may be able to approach the subject with automatic credentials and knowledge. Dr. Laura Schlessinger reaches many radio listeners via her program, offering psychological advice in response to their questions. This makes her a natural to write pop psychology books like *Ten Stupid Things Women Do to Mess Up Their Lives* and *Ten Stupid Things Men Do to Mess Up Their Lives*. In other words, she is able to bring automatic credentials to the writing desk for this type of book.

Fashion designers, real estate professionals, health and fitness experts, well-known business managers, and a long list of others have immediate credentials for doing one or more nonfiction books on subjects related to their vocations. You may have specialized knowledge or information on a subject, and this background might enable you to write a worthy nonfiction book. Search your mind. Clues may lie in hobby interests, civic work you do, or even your personal life—how you and your spouse saved your marriage, for example. The point is that the world is filled with a limitless variety of people and no two are exactly alike. Each person has his or her expertise. An inventive writer knows how to tap this peculiarity and turn it into an attractive book proposal.

It isn't a must that you be a recognized authority or expert on a subject, but any credentials you have will influence a publisher in reaching a decision on your book project.

Nonfiction Books Outsell Most Novels

Novels don't often sell as well as nonfiction, with the exception of paperback reprints of blockbuster mass-market novels. If it's a first novel, many publishers are happy to get their investment back plus a small profit. Naturally, there are books that break the general rule. Sometimes a novel will catch on no matter who wrote it (unknowns included), and even if it is the author's first book.

Consider the following:

- A successful nonfiction book can sell 100,000 copies and more. If a novel sells 35,000 or 50,000 copies, it's a bestseller and a lucky one. A lot of novels fail to sell more than 5,000 copies.

- A nonfiction book may help many readers in some practical way by teaching, informing, entertaining, or inspiring them. Such books can change lives for the better.

- Anne Fletcher's *Eating Thin for Life* was taken by Book-of-the-Month Club for a hefty advance. The promise of help is clear in the title.

- The truth is very often much more interesting to read than the product of a novelist's imagination. In other words, truth is stranger, and often more fascinating, than fiction.

- The odds of writing a bestseller are more favorable for nonfiction than for a novel.

- Nonfiction books often have a longer shelf life in bookstores, and stay in print longer, than many novels. If new novels don't start selling fast (the first several weeks to a month), many disappear from the bookstores.

Your Odds Are Better for a Nonfiction Bestseller

Look at it this way: An author is more likely to earn a lot on a book that keeps selling for years. Take that perennial favorite *The Joy of Cooking*, for example. With sales way up in the multimillions, this great book just keeps on churning out sales. Most authors would rather have one of these than twenty "also-ran" novels. Think of the millions of families and housewives who have been helped by this backlist classic.

With one or more nonfiction books to your credit, and hopefully doing well for you, you can then try your hand at a novel in between nonfiction books. Some authors discover they can do both, though many others will lean toward one of the two.

Nonfiction Offers Subject Variety

The choice of things to write about is endless and this is one of the great appeals of nonfiction for authors. At this writing, parenting books are hot, as are fitness, investing, the Internet, computer programming, money management, retirement, and home repair. The variety of subject matter from which to choose is stimulating: the state of society, biographies of the famous and infamous, the stock market, travel books, humor works, ways to a happier marriage, patriotism, divorce, sex, and on through a long list of potential topics.

Consider the variety of the following published books:

Angela's Ashes

The Royals

Talking to Heaven

When Work Doesn't Work Anymore: Women, Work, and Identity

Niagara: A History of the Falls

After Man

The Eternal Journey: How Near-Death Experiences Illuminate Our Earthly Lives

Fifty Years of Europe: An Album

Hitler's Silent Partners: Swiss Banks, Nazi Gold and the Pursuit of Justice

Maximizing the Arthritis Cure

Dining with the Duchess
The Mythology of Dogs
Bouncing Back
The Millionaire Next Door
Sources of Strength
Simple Abundance: A Daybook of Comfort and Joy
Chicken Soup for the Soul
The Superwoman Syndrome
Men Are from Mars, Women Are from Venus
The Sales Manager's Portable Answer Book
Best Boss, Worst Boss
Swim with the Sharks without Being Eaten Alive
Committed to Memory: One Hundred Best Poems to Memorize
Marie Curie: A Life
Killing Us Softly: Romance and Rebellion in Advertising
The Death Zone

The Truth About Writing a Bestseller

Banish from your mind the idea that one must be a genius to write a bestseller. It just isn't true. Most major publishers are looking for the next megabook, and they could care less if the author is experienced or not. The fact is that some debut authors are making stunning entrances into the marketplace. The following realities should encourage you:

- About 60,000 new books are published each year. Of this total, the number of really fine books is a great deal smaller.

- It is tougher to pull off, but some first-time authors manage to create a bestseller. Steven Alten's first novel, *Meg*, relates the discovery of a huge prehistoric shark in the deep of the Marianas Trench off Guam. So far, this thriller has been published in nine countries.

- When James L. Halperin embarked on a writing career, he had no idea that his first novel, *The Truth Machine*, would go on to become a national science-fiction bestseller.

- A bestseller can cover any one of a variety of subjects.

- Many terrific books are written by authors over forty and also by authors in their twenties. No one is too young or too old to hit it big, providing the writer creates the right book at the right time.

- Many top sellers are written in the home of the author as well as also in hotel rooms, cabins, cottages by the sea, formal office settings, and even bedrooms with just the mattress as a desk.

- Imaginative publicity and promotion are what often boost a book into a star seller. Certainly, they help.

- If you have an appealing, attention-holding story to tell, but you can't write very well, editors will work with you. Publishing companies are geared to handle this and help an author—within reason—if they like the story enough. The classic example of this is Thomas Wolfe's *Look Homeward, Angel* manuscript, which was over a thousand pages—a sea of words—when he brought it to legendary editor Max Perkins. It was painful for Wolfe to cut his manuscript, but that is exactly what he and Perkins did over a considerable period of time.

Bestseller Realities

A study of authors and novelists reveals that many, including the star names, have to do a lot of writing before they get that big book. A good example is Barbara Taylor Bradford. Over a six-year period, she started four novels but discarded them all after a few hundred pages. She asked herself what she really wanted to write most and decided that it was a book about a girl in Yorkshire, England, who builds an enormous business empire.

The result was *A Woman of Substance,* a very successful book. In Bradford's view, "A story is only interesting if it's about people, their tragedies, dramas, their joys."

Once they have had their first novels published, numerous authors have revealed that they wrote or experimented with one or more previous novels. Few are fortunate enough to sell the first work they fin-ish. Generally, it takes a period of time for a new author to learn the craft. Many publishing veterans refer to this as "paying your dues," and for most authors who enter the publishing gates, this is exactly what happens.

In the words of Bradford, "A novel is a monumental lie that has to have the absolute ring of truth if it is to succeed." To achieve that vital "ring of truth" takes time. For most authors, it can't be dashed off in a few months.

Look at it this way: you have the chance to produce a bestseller on your very first try, but it's usually a slim chance. If you fall short of your goal, you may have at least a mini-bestseller. If not, then your first book, whatever it sells, can pave the way for a bestseller on your second or third effort. Many wise authors are content to simply do all in their power to write the best book they can and don't even think about the bestseller lists.

Producing a Bestseller

Keep in mind that the only way a book is ever written is by someone sitting down and doing it. Still, it stands to reason that the more thought given to your novel or nonfiction book the better it will be. Some authors believe in elaborate planning while others simply write a first sentence and go from there. Ask some bestselling authors how they do it, and many reply that "you have to live with your characters and get to know them so well that you're able to bring them to life on the printed page." Authors usually have someone in mind when they create their lead characters, and this may help a book to be more believable. When writing a novel, spend a great deal of effort and time with your main character.

Bestselling author Clive Cussler, creator of the enormously suc-cessful Dirk Pitt sea-going series, and a superb storyteller, says, "You have to come up with a riveting concept for a novel." The same is basically true if nonfiction is your main interest. You need a strong idea, something fresh with wide appeal, a book that will hook readers and lots of them. There is already a glut of boring books on ho-hum subjects that don't hold enough interest for most readers. Remember that you're always competing with television, the big screen, and other forms of entertainment and recreation.

It may interest you to know that in the United States the average age at which a novelist is first published is forty, and the novel that sees print is the third written. A creative-writing professor in Canada has reportedly written forty novels with only one published to date.

Where Bestsellers Are Written

Many new authors believe they need a resortlike place or atmosphere in which to produce their books. The truth is that a bestseller can be written just about anywhere. James Michener wrote many of his finest books in a cabin. One author who turns out textbooks spends summers in London, working much of the time in British libraries.

In time, most authors discover where they can do their best work, whether it's at home, in a rented office, at the seashore, in the woods in a cabin, or locked up in a hotel room. Some lucky authors are able to write anywhere and everywhere. Others must stick to one or a few basic locations. Until you learn where the words flow best for you, simply experiment with different places.

Margaret Mitchell wrote at home. So did Hemingway for a number of his works. After his work in Hollywood, Faulkner also wrote at home. Some authors do work on airplanes, typing away on their laptop computers and jotting in notebooks. Still others use a combination of places to get words down on paper.

Imaginative Publicity and Promotion Make Bestsellers

One of the clearest realities in today's book business is the fact that authors with charisma and media appeal can turn their books into blockbusters. A single guest spot on *Today, Oprah Winfrey, Good Morning America, Tonight Show with Jay Leno,* or *Late Night with David Letterman* can send sales of a book soaring.

Believe it. Learning how to be an effective guest on local or national programs is well worth the time and effort. Some authors discover they have media charisma and are quite effective. Others need media grooming.

One definite way to a bestseller (it's worked for many) is to get out there and promote your book yourself. Authors cannot depend on their publishers to promote their books beyond some initial efforts when the books are published. The reason for this is that there are simply too many books. By the time some books are published, the publicity team and rights people are already focused on other even newer books.

If you have the time to do it, and you click with bookstore people and radio/television personalities, there is a chance your book can take off through your own promotion efforts. One thing is certain: with close to 60,000 new books coming out each year, your own promotion actions will probably give your book a far greater chance to go somewhere. Some publishers are more interested in promoting than others, so it will depend on which companies you deal with and what they are willing to do in the way of promotion and publicity. The important point is that many fine books die on the vine because of little or no promotion. Keep in mind that the best kind of advertising is word of mouth, which alone has made a number of books bestsellers.

Some authors prefer to stay in their ivory towers and do nothing but write. They don't care much for promotion trips or media interviews. But that's what sells books today. A wise author will do everything possible to help a new work sell and keep on selling. If the book is really good, and enough people hear about it, there is a good chance for word-of-mouth advertising to support your book and make its sales skyrocket.

It is not unusual for authors to want to forget their books once they are published and in the stores. They're eager to turn to new projects, yet this is when they should be doing everything possible to promote the new book with the cooperation of their publisher. The best publicity and promotion campaigns begin long before publication day.

It makes sense that your chances of having a bestseller are much better if you can develop a media personality. Most authors can't start with a guest spot on the *Today* show, but it is not too difficult to get booked on local radio and television shows. If at all possible, load your car with copies of your new book and take off on a cross-country trip, promoting it at bookstores, on local talk shows, and everywhere possible.

With enough local exposure, especially in key areas, your book sales should increase. If that continues, it can mean more enthusiasm and willingness by your publisher to do more promotion.

Additional Truths About Writing a Bestseller

When it comes to advice on creating a bestseller, you can never get enough! Here are a few more thoughts on writing books that sell:

- Views vary on how many sales mean a bestseller. Generally speaking, most consider any book with 40,000–100,000 copies (or more) sold to be a bestseller.

- If you can write a clear and effective sentence, and are willing to do the work involved in completing a book, there is always the chance your book will make it through the publishing process in good shape and carve a worthy place for itself in the marketplace. Never forget this. Even with every bad break against them, some books defy the odds and still become bestsellers, amazing all the experts in the process.

- Whenever you read a book, hear about one, or look at a bestseller in the stores, think about the concept behind it. Why is it so popular? Is it a timely subject? How was the cover promise delivered? Does the author have immediate name recognition? Break down the reasons for a book's success; then try to integrate these qualities into your own books.

- Remember always that word of mouth has turned many a book into a blockbuster. It's a fact that people who buy and like a book tell their friends, neighbors, associates, and relatives about it. The word spreads and sales keep climbing. Get the potentially endless chain of word-of-mouth publicity going for your book; at least, do all you can to trigger it.

- Keep the faith in yourself and your book, for without it nothing else really matters. If and when your book is rejected by a publisher, don't throw in the towel. There are many other publishers.

- Revisions are an absolute must for any hope of a bestseller. When publishing companies pour money into producing and marketing a title that has the potential of being a bestseller it is inevitable that the original manuscript will be put through the ringer. The hands of many skilled "professionals" will examine, mark up, advise, and revise your work until, finally, a polished title makes its way off the press. The revision process is inevitable.

- Keep in mind that publishers and editors sometimes make mistakes. A number of top-selling books were rejected many times.

- It is entirely possible to publish a bestseller without an agent, but a worthy agent can help you place the book sooner. The wrong agent, on the other hand, could hurt your career, or possibly discourage you when more writing or a revision might be enough to land you on the bestseller lists. Some reports claim that 90 percent of all trade books are submitted to publishers by agents. Many authors, however, do very well representing themselves. The time to think about an agent is after you have attained some success. Most of the better agents won't consider you until then anyway. A number of authors use an agent for fiction but place their nonfiction books on their own. You will have to decide what is best when the time comes.

- The public's fancy can change very quickly. You have just as good a chance to spot a trend developing as anyone else. In fact, newcomers often hit at just the right time with refreshing new books.

- It's far wiser to send your book manuscript to a specific editor rather than sending it unsolicited to a publisher's address. The latter method will land it in the slush pile where it may be eventually read or find its way to oblivion. Don't take that chance; address your work to a specific editor at the publishing house you believe is best suited to do your book. Two popular

resources can help you find contact information on editors and publishers: *Literary Market Place*, published by R. R. Bowker, 121 Chanlon Road, New Providence, NJ 07974, phone (800) 521-8110, fax (908) 665-6688; and *The Writer's Market*, published by F&W Publications, 1507 Dana Avenue, Cincinnati, OH 45207, phone (513) 531-2222. Another good source is *Writer's Digest*, P.O. Box 2124, Harlan, IA 51593-2313, the world's largest magazine for writers.

CHAPTER 8

Prep Work:
What Smart Writers Do
to Become Great Authors

The most fascinating thing about the book business, and being an author, is the simple truth that anything can happen.

What does it mean to make a living as a writer? The key word is "production." Most professional writers have no trouble generating ideas; the problem is finding enough time to develop the ideas that interest them most.

A workable and realistic production plan is a must, but you first need to find your special branch or book category. The majority of romance authors, for example, are women. They specialize in this field and build a track record of published books. One romance novel leads to another.

The only way to find your specialty is to experiment by writing different types of books. You might try a general-interest book or even a novel. It's up to you. Once you find your niche, you can put down roots and feel like you know at last where you belong in the industry and the type of book you want to focus on most.

Consistent Daily Work

Whatever category you choose, or even if every book you write is different, consistent daily work is a must. Most authors have daily goals of a specific number of words or pages to be written, and they are very serious about it.

Writing for a living also means plenty of revision, bouncing ideas off editors, planning, writing, and selling new proposals (or outlines and chapters). It also means promoting your books after they are published, getting publicity for them, media attention via radio and television interviews, and going to bat for your books in every way possible.

Discipline is important because a writer must be able to continually coordinate all the above activities and provide time for them.

Are You a Budding Novelist?

There are people who have never put a pen to paper, for any long work, who think they can turn out a work of fiction. You meet them at parties and banquets and hear them say, "I'm thinking of starting a novel over the weekend."

F. Scott Fitzgerald said it well: "A novel takes time." Any book does. It also takes advance thinking, planning, research, and often years of investigation. Robert Benchley, the famous and beloved humorist, once remarked on the time needed to develop writing ability: "It took me fifteen years to discover I had no talent for writing, but I couldn't give it up because by that time I was too famous."

A clue about your writing potential lies in what you like to read best. Fiction or nonfiction? That is the question. If you like to read novels, then you may well prefer writing them. There's no rule on this written in stone, but, generally speaking, to write the type book you enjoy reading is a sound decision.

Demystifying the Creative Process

The late Paul Francis Webster, a three-time Academy Award-winning songwriter, once said that two of the most creative places he knew of were "on a train from Los Angeles to New York and at the top of the

highest hill in Hong Kong." It is very true that certain places stimulate the creative juices more than others.

Creative people ask questions. What if I switched things around? How about an overseas setting for this story or book? Could a key element from one work be shifted to another? The creative process thrives on experimentation, first trying one thing and then another. Thomas Edison, creative genius that he was, was never despondent throughout the ten thousand attempts it took to find the solution that would allow him to produce electric light. Edison's reaction was direct and simple: "We know this idea won't work so that means we're just one step closer to finding what will work." Eventually, he invented a filament that became the solution for the electric lightbulb.

Everything Starts with an Idea

Think about it. Everything starts with an idea: paintings, cars, songs, new airplane designs, buildings, and great books.

Developing an idea is where work and time come into the picture. When you go with an idea, it may carry you to unknown areas, to the heights of satisfaction or to the depths of depression if you get bogged down with it.

In the superb novel *The Fountainhead* by Ayn Rand, architect Howard Roark states that "the creative artist has a unique right to the original ideas he produces and develops. Others cannot make use of this creative work without agreement and compensation."

What is reflected in *The Fountainhead* is the truth that "everything is built upon something else in creation." Play with a single basic idea and what happens? More ideas present themselves to you.

The act of creating means the ability to shift qualities or elements from one thing to another. Hollywood has been doing this for decades, lifting (some say stealing) a key element from an old classic film and building a new film from or around it.

The creative process takes varying amounts of time, depending upon the desired result. A book obviously takes much longer to create than an article, short story, or song. There are exceptions to this when you consider prolific authors like Barbara Cartland and the late

Isaac Asimov. They could turn out a new book in a week and often did so. Cartland continues her amazing prolific work.

Creative ideas may evolve into creative problems—real puzzlers for their originators. The ideas then require much more thought and effort to work their way through the sticky areas. The great literary talent Gene Fowler summed up the task of writing by saying, "Writing is easy. All you have to do is sit staring at a blank sheet of paper until the drops of blood form on your forehead." Thomas Edison spent ten, twenty years and longer on some of his creative inventions; writers must keep in mind that their best work may take as long to perfect.

How to Plan and Organize Your Research

Good authors thoroughly research their book ideas. Here are some guidelines on doing research for the book (or books) you're planning to write. The list is by no means complete. If you are new to research, your librarian can be a big help.

1. Some very useful tools that you will want on hand for your writing include *Elements of Style*, *The Chicago Manual of Style*, and *Words into Type*. They will help you to write well and style your manuscript in a manner that will appear professional to publishers.

2. *Books in Print* is an absolute must for researching what other books have been published on any subject you may be considering. It will give you a continuous list of the new works coming out each year. Publishers often ask about competitive books, and knowing the competition can help you decide if an idea is worth pursuing.

3. Begin your book project with some background reading or even a lot of it. If your work is a novel, read about the time period in which your story takes place, e.g., the Victorian period, the eighteenth century, World War II, or the Civil War. For nonfiction, be certain to read as many other books written on the subject as possible. This includes new and old books plus articles in magazines, newspapers, and booklets.

4. Some authors make notes while reading and record them on index cards for later reference. Others prefer to use legal pads or elaborate notebooks.

5. If your work is a historical novel, you will find it very important to make a list or sketch of the key events in which you want your characters involved.

6. When you know the time and place for your novel, you will find that certain biographies and histories of the era paint a good picture. They will be of enormous help to you.

7. Don't overlook diaries of the period about which you are writing. Diaries have been kept since writing was invented and are very useful for adding details about various time periods, including what people were thinking about, the politics and customs, fashions, and popular songs and books of the era.

8. Government sources are a gold mine for authors. Never overlook the vast materials published by the government when researching your book. There may be agencies or branches of government that can supply you with very helpful material. You can ask for this material in person or write and request it. If your book is nonfiction and will have illustrations, you may be able to obtain some excellent photos from these sources and at moderate prices.

9. Most countries have research institutes that are well worth checking out. You may obtain key information from them.

10. Personal interviews remain one of the best ways to get material for your book. People themselves are an endless source of material. Many people are flattered by an author's request for an interview, though some don't like to see a tape recorder during the interview. You can, of course, ask if they mind you taping the interview in order to be accurate. If they turn you down, at least you tried. If you must use the note method, try to get down what they tell you as accurately as possible.

11. Old letters and documents may be good sources of facts for a variety of books.

12. If at all possible, you should visit the locale you are going to write about, even if it happens to be the other side of the world. On the other hand, keep in mind that some excellent books have been written right in libraries (or the author's home) even though readers would swear the authors were actually at the scene.

Don't Waste Valuable Research Time

It does not take a genius to collect background material. Most could do it with little trouble. You want the time period in which your novel is set to be authentic. Your goal, for historical novels, is to recreate the time during which your story unfolds.

While you research a book, use your time wisely. Get an early start on those days you plan for research, and get to know some of the key people in the libraries you intend to use; they can be of great help to you.

Determine well in advance how much time you will spend on the research stage of your book. Many authors work out a schedule planning the actual time segments. This will also save you from backtracking. You will know what to do each week, where to go for certain material, and how much more you need.

Interviews Help Breathe Life into Your Ideas

Let's say you wish to write a nonfiction book about some celebrity. Tough as it may be to line up a personal interview with the person, it's worth a try. You may have to contact the celebrity's public relations agent or manager, and these people sometimes keep tight reins on their clients. Depending on luck, timing, and the current schedule of the celebrity, you may succeed in landing the interview. Your credentials and track record as an author can help plus other factors.

Some celebrities, stars, or VIP people you may wish to interview can be reached by mail. You will never know unless you try. Be sure to mention in your letter any articles or books you have had published—or anything else that is relevant.

Some of the very best and strongest material for your book can come from personal interviews. L. P. Wilbur was lucky enough to obtain an interview with Oscar-winning motion picture songwriter, Paul Frances Webster, and the resulting material became the basis for one of the strongest chapters in *How to Write Songs That Sell.* Four hours on two separate days were spent in the songwriter's Beverly Hills mansion, in the study, and it was one of the most fascinating interviews conducted by this author, who was in awe of the celebrity's three Academy Awards, numerous Grammy awards, plaques, citations, and more on display in the study.

Why are interviews so helpful? The facts and informed opinions provided by business executives, professors, politicians, and scientists, for example, can provide you, the author, with new insights, making it possible for you to write a more substantial and credible book. The quotes you get in interviews can add flavor and depth to your book. And the public enjoys reading the opinions of celebrities, stars, as well as of other famous or important people.

How to Be Ready for Every Interview

Do your homework before you interview anyone. Read about the person. Know the key facts about his or her life and consult newspaper or magazine indexes for further information. This advance reading and preparation will help you a lot during the interview and will make it go much more smoothly. The person you are interviewing will also know if you did your homework.

Prepare a list of the questions you intend to ask during each interview. Do this whether or not the person is famous. Knowing what you will ask saves time and usually elicits the specific material you can use. Strive for accuracy in getting the answers, that is, quotes that convey the precise information you are looking for.

The Benefits of Research

You will write a better book if you do the research. Here are a number of reasons for doing it well:

- The right kind of research helps you to sense what must be said in the book.

- You discover and uncover important facts for your book.

- The result of important research can mean a greater demand for your book. The new information you present may have a far-reaching influence on readers.

- Your finished book (or books) is more significant and up-to-date with fresh information and quotes.

- The research you do for historical and other novels can help catapult your books onto the bestseller lists.

- Many authors come across ideas and material for their next books while engaged in original research. You may reap the same rewards.

- Research adds power and interest, color, reality, accuracy, believability, and the stuff of life itself to novels and nonfiction books.

- Doing research for a book is fascinating for a great many authors. Some hate it; others love it and thrive on it. Beware of one pitfall: spending too much time on research and making it an end in itself. Don't fall into this trap, because the fascination and joys of research can consume you and the time you should be spending on writing. Strong research brings books to life. Thoughtful and imaginative research lets the reader know that the author has done his or her homework. The resulting book (or books) has substance and value.

CHAPTER 9

———◆———

The Blank Page
Comes to Life

Bringing a book to life is an exciting adventure. Make no mistake about it. Creating a book from nothing is similar, in a sense, to child-birth. Whether it sells a million copies or only five thousand, there is something very satisfying, even mystical, about bringing a new book into the world.

A book is a one-on-one experience. It is your words, ideas, and thoughts being communicated to the minds and hearts of readers you will never meet personally. Yet, in the pages of your book, you do meet the reader. You lead the reader on a journey from page one to the last word. Each reader of your book shares a part of his or her life with the story or material of your book.

When It's Time to Start the Writing

When the first page looms before you, and it's time to start the writ-ing, some important questions to ask (if you have not already done so) are as follows: How can I say what I want to without boring the reader? How can I make the reader care about my characters and the situations in which they are involved? How can I entertain or instruct the reader of this book?

One very helpful guideline is not to let all the material you have researched or gathered scare you. If the book you want to write is your first, or twentieth, don't be overwhelmed by the mountain of facts and material you have gathered and worry about transferring it into a book.

Worry about how to get it into book pages and you will be constantly on edge. Instead, follow these simple directions: realize first that you don't have to use all of the material you have; go instead with the cream-of-the-crop. If you already have an outline, you will have a map, a framework showing where your material will be used. Your mountain of material will soon start to shrink by separating it into the key sections or divisions of your book. This process will become clear to you by simply sorting through your material.

Get a handle on the beginning, middle, and ending of your book. Put your material into the proper divisions. Then the mountain you first had in front of you will have shrunk to a molehill.

Discipline is vitally important for an author. Some authors sign book contracts, receive and spend their advances, and then never complete the books they agreed to do. Publishers have been burned by such authors, and this is a key reason they look for assurances that a given author, known or unknown, will actually finish a manuscript.

Discipline will help you finish your book (or books). Without enough discipline, you may never reach that final book page. Try to develop as much working discipline as possible, for it can play a major role in leading you to success.

Finding the Right Place and Time to Write

If you have a daily job, it's clear that the only time you will have for your writing is either early in the morning or in the evening. You may be too exhausted in the evening, so that leaves the morning as probably your best time.

You need some time for recreation and plain relaxation. Many authors find their best time for work by experimenting with different schedules. You should do the same. You could, for example, get in two hours of writing in the early morning hours before going to your job. An advantage to doing work in the morning is that your mind is fresh. Many authors have turned out fine books using such a schedule.

Another option is working from eight or nine at night to midnight. A worthy and realistic goal is about three hours a day at least for your writing. If there is no way you can devote a block of three hours a day to writing, then you will have to settle for an hour or so in the morning and one or two at night. You should try both.

It is vitally important that you work in the same place and at the same time each day. At least, most authors believe this is important. Your mind will learn that you mean to work at that time and in that place. Training your mind in good work habits is very helpful. The mind becomes used to a routine and cooperates better than it would if you wrote at a different time and place each day. Some lucky authors can write no matter where they are or what time of day or night it is. John O'Hara, who was very successful, wrote all night.

Some authors work hard Monday through Friday and then totally relax during the weekend. Others work the same hours at their writing desk seven days a week. Some authors don't go on clock time; they set a certain number of pages to do per day as a goal. Some days they may get their pages early, but on others it may take them more than the time they have allotted themselves. Three or four pages a day is a realistic goal for many authors. Others go for more. George Sand's thirty pages a night was incredible, but one wonders how many pages of that output had to be thrown out.

A long break from your writing routine may cause difficulty in getting started again. There are natural rhythms in writing. This is one reason why many authors like to work every day when doing a book. A week or two away from writing, or even a weekend, may interrupt your normal rhythm or cycle.

The optimal place for you to write will also come by experimenting. Some authors rent hotel rooms without windows so there are no distractions. They even remove the telephones. You can try your kitchen table, a desk in a study, a formal office, the seashore, a cabin in the mountains, or wherever. Go with wherever the words seem to flow best. Remember that Mario Puzo wrote *The Godfather* at his kitchen table. Other authors have written on coffee tables while sitting on the carpet, or on airplanes, boats, trains, and other places. Just go with the place you like best.

The First Page Is the Hardest

Perhaps it's psychological, but there is something about completing a first page that often sets everything in motion. The inertia has been overcome, and the words start to flow, sometimes like a sweeping tide. Some authors get bogged down in those first few pages, but for many, completing the first page acts as an incentive to continue. After all, with the first page done, you have proved to yourself that you can make a start on a book.

In other words, for a great many authors, page one has a way of growing into five, ten, or twenty pages. Sooner or later, you realize that those pages have combined to produce a chapter or section of your book. That can be a great feeling.

Some authors are simply stimulated by a blank page. They warm to the idea of all that white space to be filled with words, sentences, and paragraphs. Others may stare in horror for hours or days at the blank page before them. One person makes an easy start, while another author finds it painful or difficult to write. You will soon discover your type or if you are somewhere between the two. Once writing has you hooked, the need to write will drive you regardless of whether or not it comes easy.

A clue that you have true writing ability lies in the blank white paper. Do you like the feel of it in your hands? If so, it could be a sign that you are in the right work. Even older, established authors with many years of experience behind them still get a thrill from handling blank paper, pens, and pencils, and now word processors and computers in all their shapes and sizes. Mystical? Perhaps, or maybe the sign of a born writer.

Most books, novels or nonfiction, require advance thinking and preparation. Here is a checklist of some things to consider before starting your first chapter. Use the ones that seem right for you.

NONFICTION BOOKS

- Research, reading, and interviews completed. The time needed for research varies from several weeks to years, depending on what you are writing.
- Outline written with all changes to date included.
- Subheadings or sections planned; chapter titles ready.
- Special examples, anecdotes, and quotations selected.

NOVELS

- Theme of novel stated in a short sentence.
- Decision made for setting and time of the story.
- Statement of the conflict of the novel and its resolution.
- Chart or table of characters written, along with a clear description of each (age, appearance, traits, motivations). Many authors complete a sketch for each character.
- Breakdown made of the scenes or action of the first chapter. Some novelists plan chapters one at a time, as they come to them. Others block out the entire book, and still others work with no plan at all.

The Importance of a Strong Introduction

The opening pages of your book are vitally important. They must grab the reader's attention quickly and hold it. Many browsers in bookstores turn to the first page or introduction of the book. If they like what they read, they may decide to buy it then and there. If they're bored by what they read, or the material has little interest or promise of being a good read, they will replace the book on the shelf and reach for another one.

Here are some useful questions to ask yourself when planning the introduction for your book:

- What can I open with in my book that will hook the reader's attention?

- Is there some dramatic or surprise beginning I could use?
- Would a key question get attention?
- How can I make my introduction for this book different and especially appealing?

Study and read carefully the introductions used by other writers for their books. Make notes of the strong openings, the dynamic attention-getters, and why you think they were successful. A number of nonfiction books don't have an introduction, but stay on the lookout for those that make use of an effective beginning.

Promise Yourself Little Rewards

Lots of smart authors get more work accomplished, or make their current projects go more smoothly, by treating themselves to little rewards now and then. These vary from taking a ten-minute break after finishing several pages or a certain segment of work, to relaxing in front of the television set for a while. Set a timer or, before you know it, the whole evening will be gone, annihilated by TV. Television can steal your valuable time quicker than a pickpocket can steal your wallet in a crowded circus. Remember always: the most valuable thing an author has is time. Make the best possible use of it.

One writer may take a day off after completing a chapter. Another will spice up the workday with a quick snack or coffee breaks. Some authors work like beavers Monday through Friday and relax over the weekend; others work in spurts and then knock off for a day or so. There are many writers who almost never quit. They're working all the time; if they're not writing, they're involved in research, interviewing, planning, or some other work-related activity.

Someone once wrote that "the true author works constantly throughout his or her career." In the sense that most authors think about their work a great deal, even when actively engaged in some other activity, this is true. Writers can't seem to shut it off; the process is going on within them constantly. Many authors seem to be happiest when they're working on books. Some achieve enough money and success to relax a bit, but continue writing for its own sake.

Some writers say they experience a terrible letdown after a book is completed, a sort of postpartum depression. It's a trying time for them. They're depressed when the work on one project comes to an end and they're ready and anxious to get on with their next book. In truth, writing breeds more writing. For most authors, the more writing they do, the more they want to do.

Chapters Make Your Book

It may sound obvious, but try to keep one fact about writing books in mind at all times: chapters make your book. This basic truth can help you finish any number of projects.

Chapters are the framework of your book. You can sustain your enthusiasm by realizing that you draw ever nearer to its completion with every new chapter you finish. Don't underestimate this truth. Many people who consider writing a book never do it. An important reason why they never do is that the thought of all the work involved scares them. It can be frightening to think of the work required for a book, regardless of the length.

So, don't let your book project leer at you with its length, scope, or amount of work needed to become a reality. Seeing all that work—in one massive dose—can depress even the most prolific of authors. Your salvation lies in chapters. By breaking the total project down, you're not overwhelmed by the sheer magnitude of it. You may not see how your book will end, or even see its middle part. Don't worry about it. Just concentrate on doing one chapter at a time. Give your attention to the chapter at hand. When you're satisfied with it, move on to the next. Chapters have a marvelous way of adding up, just as pages do.

Focus on the bits and pieces of your project—the words, sentences, paragraphs, pages, and chapters. These will all work together to produce the beginning, middle, and end of your book. Look at it this way: if you wrote just one page a day for the next year, you would have a book of 365 pages. Or you could do the same by writing two pages a day for six months. The work schedule you set and stick to is up to you.

Advance Planning Pays Off

Authors develop various ways to keep making progress on their books. Some authors, for example, plan their next chapter whenever they find themselves bogged down with a current one. This way, they don't lose valuable time.

A lot of writers work hard on the advance planning of chapters. Such work pays off when they are ready to begin the actual writing of the book. After you complete chapter one, you already have a script for chapter two and know where you're heading with the material. That's the result of advance planning. It keeps your progress moving forward smoothly and continually.

Advance planning of chapters can be another source of enthusiasm. You're eager to get into the next chapter because the plan for it is ready and waiting. The total effort results in increased confidence as your book comes to life.

Chapter Headings Stimulate Your Writing

While some novels don't have any chapter headings, most nonfiction books make use of them. Chapter headings can even increase the sales of your book. Watch how many browsers and customers in bookstores skim through books, glancing at the chapter headings. Many will decide to buy a particular book if the chapter headings offer the promise of good reading.

What is more important is the fact that well-written chapter headings stimulate your writing all through your book. Some will interest you more than others, but all of them act as signals. They tell what each chapter is about and what the reader is likely to find there.

Vary the Lengths of Your Chapters

Never forget that all readers are human. Give them some variety in the length of your chapters. Don't follow a long one with too many others of the same length. Break up the pace now and then.

If properly placed in a book, short chapters provide relief and help the readers feel that they are making progress in finishing the book. No one likes to feel that reading is a chore. In other words, make the reading journey as easy and clear as possible.

Readers often take a rest or refreshment break after finishing a chapter. If many of your chapters are too long, your readers may have to stop in the middle or end of a page in order to take their breaks.

Most people enjoy variety in the books they read. No author can ever be certain that those who buy a book will read it straight through at one sitting. It's nice to think that at least some people might do so. But reading habits, along with comprehension levels, differ. So, help the reader along with variety in your chapter length, style, and presentation.

Some Chapters Are Tougher Than Others

Any author worth the title knows from experience that some chapters are harder to write than others. It's par for the course.

Whether you write one book or twenty, you'll soon discover this for yourself. Some chapters almost write themselves. The work seems to flow. The material seems fresh and vibrant. The writer is enthusiastic and may even feel sad to reach the end of such chapters.

Not so with other chapters. Any author may get stuck at any point. If and when this happens to you, don't force it. If you get bogged down, try one of the following remedies:

1. Take a break. Relax and think about something else for a while. You will come back refreshed and better able to solve the problem.
2. Liquid refreshment may help. Drink a soda, cup of coffee, tea, or a glass of fruit juice. Nothing stronger. Remember, you're writing. Liquor and writing don't mix well.
3. Take a brisk walk for thirty minutes or so.
4. Try reading the material out loud. This can help.
5. If nothing seems to work, knock off work for a few hours or even until the next day.

Once they have their book outlines, some writers go through them and mark the chapters they feel will be most interesting or easiest to write, and those that will be the toughest. Then they can alternate between difficult writing, first completing an easy or interesting chapter, followed by a tougher one. Some authors, of course, find every chapter hard to write, while the lucky ones enjoy working on every single part of their books.

Chapter One Sets the Theme of Your Book

I hope you already realize the importance of the first chapter. This is your grand opening. The spotlight is on your first sentences. The reader's attention is focused on your words. In the case of novels, the first few paragraphs may well determine whether your book sells. Remember, many a prospective book buyer will read the first page before making a decision to buy or not.

The opening paragraph should be strong enough to grab the reader's attention and say, "Hey, there, you with the bloodshot eyes. Buy me. I'm good reading. You won't be able to put me down."

The first chapter often influences a buying decision—don't underestimate its pulling power. In addition to reading the introduction, prospective buyers of nonfiction may read half or more of the first chapter before deciding whether or not to buy. This is especially true if the opening chapter is fairly short.

The first chapter also sets the tone and establishes the theme, or purpose, of your book. If sent with an outline to an editor, your first chapter can mean the difference between the sale of your work or its prompt return to you. No wonder many authors rewrite their first chapters several times. They know it's *that* important.

Make Your Last Chapter as Good as the First

Some writers are so glad to reach the last chapter in their books that they're tempted to rush through it as quickly as possible. This is a mistake.

A sound rule for writing books that will sell is to do all in your power to make your last chapter just as strong as the opening one. Actually, this rule should apply to every chapter. Put your heart into each one and you'll never feel sorry later that you didn't give a particular chapter your most serious effort.

Remember, it's too late after your book is in print. Once published, that's it until a future edition, if any, is published—and that may never happen. So, do your best all the way through your book. Then you will have the satisfaction of knowing that your best possible efforts went into writing an effective and worthwhile book.

Whether your book sells 5,000 copies or 100,000, you'll take pride in the knowledge that you gave your project all you possibly could. Who could ask for anything more?

What About Length?

The length of a book can have an influence on a buying decision. You can prove this to yourself by watching browsers in bookstores examine the thickness of a book before or after noting the price.

People in general do tend to feel that a $25 or $30 book should offer a suitable thickness. Many book buyers forget that it's not how many pages in a book that matter most, but what's on those pages. Obviously, a big-name author may get away with a shorter book. The name recognition makes up for the price. But the average book buyer thinks seriously before spending $25 for a hardcover or $10 or more for a paperback.

Many business and professional books are priced over $25–$30, so the size of these books may be carefully noted by a number of buyers. The majority of book buyers probably feel they are getting their money's worth if the size of the books they are considering is commensurate with the asking price.

Nonfiction books run from about 50,000 to 80,000 words in most cases. Paperback originals run from a short 30,000 words to 50,000 words and up. Adventure books and some romances may run 100,000 words and over. Saga type novels tend to run 500 pages and more. Juveniles and young adult books usually run from about 40,000 to 50,000 words.

Some novels dictate their own length. Novels run from about one hundred pages to over one thousand. Family-saga novels usually run much longer than general novels. You will find the following estimates on various novel lengths useful:

Book Length (Fiction)

General novels:	100–400 pages. Many general novels run about 200 pages.
Family sagas:	500–1,000 pages
Romance novels:	200–300 pages
Adventure novels:	200–300 pages
Mystery novels:	200 pages
Miscellaneous books:	100–200 pages
Average length:	200–250 pages

Nonfiction books can run anywhere from 100 pages up to 1,000 and more. Note that these estimates are for printed pages. A normal double-spaced manuscript will normally run longer than the printed book, usually by about one half.

Do not think that a book must be a thousand pages or more to become a bestseller. Short books have also done well in the marketplace. They will most probably continue to do well, and perhaps even better, in the twenty-first century.

A number of book buyers make their decisions to buy a book on pure impulse. If a given book strikes a browser's fancy, he or she may buy it, regardless of the length. In truth, from the writer's point of view, each book tends to forge its own length. Just write until the story or material reaches a conclusion that is satisfying and logical.

If you plan to write more than one book in the future, a good general rule is to not limit yourself to any certain length. Shoot for a variety of lengths. Your first book, for example, might run about 150 pages. Your second one could be shorter or longer. In the course of your writing, you will probably create long and short works. Both can appeal to the public and become bestsellers. Stephen King's *The Stand*, published by Doubleday in 1978, was 823 pages long. Conversely, Richard Bach's classic, *Jonathan Livingston Seagull*, reissued by Macmillan in 1997, is only 93 pages long.

There are rare business and financial exceptions, of course. Sometimes publishers request that authors deliver manuscripts that fall within a specified page range, say 250–300 pages. In such cases, the publisher is either (1) making sure the manuscript is of sufficient length to drive the sale of the book once it is released or (2) making sure the manuscript isn't too long—thick books take more time to edit, cost publishers more money to print, and don't always lead to increased sales.

Unless told differently by your publisher, just let each book lead the way. It's what you say on those pages that is important. Don't worry about the length. Say what you need to say and then stop.

The Push to the Finish

A wondrous fact about writing a book is that one page leads to another. Ask authors what they like most about their work, and many will answer that the accumulation of completed pages is one of their keenest pleasures.

Bestselling author William F. Buckley once remarked: "I get pleasure out of having written. I like to paint. I don't like writing, but there is a net satisfaction when it's done. I write every day without excuse. If you put in seven days a week at 1,500 words a day, in five weeks you have a book."

What helps enormously in the push to finish a book is watching the pages grow from just a few to a hundred and then, in the home stretch, reach closer and closer to your final page. It's true that piling up pages may be harder on a first book, but the more experience you gain, the easier this push to the finish becomes. Keep in mind that some books are naturally tougher to write than others, depending on the scope of the subject and its development.

Writing the kind of book that you yourself enjoy may be the very best method for pushing through to the ending. H. G. Wells is an excellent example. Wells had a deep desire to write a novel about time travel, a desire to develop such a novel. The result was *The Time Machine.* Many a book gets abandoned in midstream because the author loses interest or grows to hate the book.

First novelists have a lot of reasons for never starting a novel, so successfully reaching the end of a work of fiction, and nonfiction, too, for that matter, depends on the author's determination. If you feel your book has to be written no matter what, the odds are good you will get to the last page of it. A case in point is Richard Bach, author of *The Bridge Across Forever* and *Jonathan Livingston Seagull*. Bach writes books that he feels have to be written. No doubt this is a big help in pushing to the end.

Remember to take advantage of cycles because your productivity is related to them. There are times when the words and chapters just seem to flow. Every author learns how to recognize these cycles and to shift into high gear when the creative juices are flowing so as to use the high point to maximum advantage. You should plan to do the same.

In time you will be able to anticipate these fortunate upswings and know in advance when one is about to begin or end. Be ready to hit your stride and get in as much work as possible. You can often double or triple your output during these highly creative periods. They are like clearings you reach in a forest. Use them wisely.

Rewriting Makes a Good Book Great

The majority of authors accept the truth that most books require some degree of revision. There just aren't too many authors who can sit down and turn out hundreds of pages of perfect prose. Rewriting is part of the trade.

Rosemary Rogers reportedly rewrote her novel *Sweet Savage Love* an incredible twenty-three times before sending it to a major New York publisher. Her book became a big bestseller and sold millions of copies.

Revision can and does improve a manuscript. Few authors have the patience to rewrite twenty-three times, or even ten, but many who earn their living by the pen believe in at least several revisions.

Some books turn out well with only slight revision. It all depends. It's true also that some authors are obsessed with revising and are never satisfied. It is possible to do too much revision. Part of the reason some authors can't let a manuscript go is fear it won't sell or that it can still be improved. There comes a point with every manuscript when it's time to let go of it and to send it on its way to market, to make its way in the world. Authors can get so close to a book that it's like parting with their baby, their child; they hate to say good-bye. Quite a few feel let down when they reach the end of a book.

Other authors are just plain arrogant, refusing to even consider revisions. A small percentage of such authors are true geniuses—they really don't need to make changes to their manuscript. The others—perhaps 95 percent of us—need some sort of guidance. Comments and revisions actually improve the quality of our books. If you're the kind of author who dislikes comments from outsiders and hates to make changes, consider self-publishing your book. That way, you don't have to dot your *i*'s and cross your *t*'s if you don't want to. You're the boss.

Novels sometimes require less revision than nonfiction books. But the reverse may also be true. In time you will be able to trust your own instincts. Something will tell you that a manuscript you have completed needs a rewrite or two more drafts. At other times you will be certain that a book you have completed needs only minor corrections.

Just because you rewrite a book three or more times is no guarantee you will have a bestseller. There are no guarantees unless you're a big-name author, a proven commodity. Still, the history of bestsellers indicates that a lot of them underwent a considerable amount of revision. Almost every book does.

A manuscript can always be improved through revision. Such effort can and does pay off for an author in terms of a better selling book and quite possibly a bestseller. John Grisham, king of the best-selling authors today, rewrites his manuscripts. So do most, if not all, of the other top author names in publishing.

There are several methods of rewriting your manuscript. You will want to try each one so you can discover which you prefer. These revision choices include the following:

1. Change and correct your work as you go along. In other words, make corrections on each page as you write it.

2. Do one or more complete rewrites of your manuscript. For many authors, the magic number of complete rewrites seems to be three.

3. After completing a first draft, go back over the complete manuscript, writing in all changes and corrections with a red pencil or pen. Then make the changes to the document.

4. Write one or more chapters and then revise them before proceeding further with your book.

Here are more guidelines, and specifics, for adding strength to your manuscript:

- Change long and confusing sentences to short clear ones. This can help just about any manuscript.

- Make paragraph transitions smoother.

- Cut technical words and replace them with simple ones.

- Cut material in a novel that does not seem to move the story along (sections that go off in other directions).

- Rewrite wordy material.

- Delete repetitious material. Don't repeat what you have already said unless you are emphasizing a point.

- Dialogue is crucial in a novel, but avoid making too much of the book into dialogue. Alternate the flow of dialogue with narrative and descriptive passages.

- Put variety in your nonfiction books. Don't present the material in the same old way.

- Shorten paragraphs that are long and rambling. Break them up into shorter- and medium-length ones.

- Check to see that there are plenty of examples and anecdotes in your nonfiction books. More can usually be added, but be selective about them.

- Limit the use of dots and dashes.

- Correct grammatical errors, spelling, and punctuation.

- Rewrite sections that don't ring true.

- Let someone you trust—an editor, an agent, another writer, or someone who knows your subject—read your manuscript, and seriously consider his or her suggestions and responses.

As long as you write, you will profit from revision. Work, patience, and revision. That's the name of the game or, rather, the names of the game.

Collaborations and Ghostwriting

When a professional author agrees to collaborate with a celebrity on a book, a commitment is usually made to do the following:

1. Work out a plan and structure for the book.
2. Ask probing questions that will bring the best responses from the expert, star, or celebrity. This helps to focus on choice material.
3. Steer the work in progress and strive to write a quality book.

When a public figure, celebrity, or film star decides to do a book, a literary agency or publisher is contacted. Then the agent or publishing house looks for the right author to work with the celebrity. There must be rapport between the two if the resulting book is to be an effective one. According to publishing executives, "Finding the right author is vital and can spell the difference between a pretty fair book and an excellent one. The decisive factor about whether we do a project is often whether or not we can get the right writer."

One author, Samm Sinclair Baker, who has done collaborative work, believes the arrangement between celebrity and author should be equal: "No partnership is any good that isn't fifty-fifty. Otherwise, the expert is saying the author is inferior."

As you have no doubt seen in many bookstores, most well-known celebrities from the entertainment industry, broadcasting, politics, the government, and business world are unable to write their own books without help. There are some exceptions. Some film stars and well-known figures have done a fine job writing their own books. Those who decide to collaborate work with professional authors. The resulting title covers read "as told to" or "with Kitty Kelly."

The point is that the authors who choose to collaborate must work out an arrangement with the expert or celebrity. There should be a written agreement on how the author is to be compensated for his or her work on the book.

Keep this idea of collaborative writing in mind. Tell editors you know, or work with in the future, of your interest in collaborative work with celebrities and public figures including film stars. If you sign with an agent for representation, let him or her know that you would be glad to consider any collaborative writing deals.

All in all, collaborative and ghostwriting have opened up additional options for today's author. Ghostwritten material can be used to showcase a writer's style. If the ghostwritten work gets published, an author can indicate this writing credit on his or her resume. Ghostwriting just might give your career a boost!

———◆———

CHAPTER 10

Creating a Book Proposal Worthy of Consideration

To outline or not? That is the question and an important one. Many authors prefer not to do one, but a promising outline can help an editor make a quick decision regarding a book.

Why a book on this subject and why should you be the one to write it? These are questions an editor will seek answers to when reading your outline. Summarize your idea or premise for the book and make a valid case for it. Provide the editor with a table of contents. This in itself will show the editor that you have the project well into the planning stage, if not further. If your outline describes and shows your plan for a book with powerful appeal, you are that much closer to a "yes" decision. Always include an outline when you send a description of a book idea.

Chapter Outlines Grab Attention

Many authors have been successful at grabbing an editor's attention via an outline. The author first sends a complete outline or perhaps merely a synopsis of the project. If and when the editor expresses interest, several sample chapters can be sent. An outline can be used as a teaser and a means of testing an editor's interest.

You'll learn with experience that requirements vary with the editor and publisher. Some editors will make a decision based on an outline alone, particularly if you have already been published. Other editors need an outline and several chapters before reaching a final decision.

If you are a new writer, with a fear or dislike for outlines, remember that some kind of plan for your book, however brief, is probably better than none at all. And that goes double if the book you want to write is nonfiction.

An Outline Can Build Enthusiasm

An outline is a road map for writing your book. This is why having an outline can keep you enthused and help get the book done. Never underestimate the power of enthusiasm. Staying excited about your book in progress is vitally important. Enthusiasm can keep you hanging in there, making decisions, thinking, writing and rewriting, and working at your desk until your book is completed.

Take the effort and time to write the best outline you can, as it will have a double payoff. It serves as a guide to what comes next, and it generates enthusiasm.

Cliché or not, it's still true that man "succeeds by bits and pieces," meaning all of us. Most humans need to see the next step in their journey toward a specific goal. An outline shows an author that next step, the next section or chapter to write.

Some nonfiction authors and novelists do not like an outline because they feel it cramps their freedom, style, or creativity. Many other authors would never think of writing a book without first doing a sound outline.

Peter Benchley sold his first novel, *Jaws*, on the basis of a one-page outline that described his idea for a book about a great white shark that terrorizes a Long Island resort. Benchley had mentioned this idea to an editor at Doubleday, and he asked to see the idea expanded. Benchley described it on paper. The editor liked the outline enough to take an option on seeing four chapters.

Jaws was finished nineteen months later and made publishing history. Here alone is vivid proof of the value of an outline.

Elements of a Book Proposal

A book proposal for nonfiction is easier to plan, write, and sell than one for fiction. The author obtains all the facts needed and goes from there. True crime, biography, a book of recipes, reference, and others— all are constructed from facts.

Book proposals that lead to publishing contracts have certain identifiable traits in common. As you learn more about each element of a book proposal, you will see how two authors—Darryl Wimberley and Jon Samsel—used them in a successful proposal for a how-to book about interactive writing.

TITLE AND TITLE PAGE

Titles by themselves cannot be copyrighted. One thing that bugs some authors is the fact that a publisher may, and usually does, change the title. An author may send in a fine title, only to see it changed. One author of this book once sent in a manuscript with the title *Is This All There Is?* Guess what the publisher did? Changed it to a how-to title not nearly as strong or on target for what the book discussed. Six months later, another book came out with the title *Is This All There Is?* It became a bestseller.

The best thing about some book proposals is the title, which could well be the strongest selling point of the book. Work hard to get a compelling, magnetic title. One way to do this is to bounce ideas off a family member, relative, friend, or other writer. Two heads are usually better than one. You can also think of possible titles when you're assembling the proposal or have the manuscript in progress.

Never underestimate the power of a strong title for a book. Editors respond to great titles. Here are a few examples:

- *Midnight in the Garden of Good and Evil*
- *Chicken Soup for the Soul*
- *The First Immortal*

- *Ten Stupid Things Women Do to Mess Up Their Lives*
- *What to Expect When You're Expecting*
- *Mutant Message Down Under*
- *Parenting Isn't for Cowards*
- *The Truth Machine*
- *The Dark Side of Camelot*
- *Bare Knuckles and Back Rooms*
- *Driving under the Affluence*
- *Men Are from Mars, Women Are from Venus*
- *A History of God*

Wimberley and Samsel decided on a strong, functional title—*Writing for Interactive Media*—rather than a flashy, more striking title (it's a nonfiction book). The book's target audience—computer professionals, academia, and students—is more impressed by rich and engaging content than a cute title.

The title page included a diagram of an interactive flowchart, the names of the authors, contact information (name, address, phone number, and e-mail address), and a copyright mark.

QUICK SUMMARY/LOG LINE

The quick summary/log line is where authors summarize their work in twenty words or less. Imagine for a moment that you are with a small gathering of friends and associates. Somebody asks you what your new book is about. Quickly, without hesitation, the following words spill forth from your lips. That's what the quick summary is all about—quickly summarizing your book in a phrase or a sentence that anyone can easily comprehend. Think of a log line as a one-sentence *TV Guide* listing.

The quick summary for Wimberley and Samsel's book, *Writing for Interactive Media*, was the following:

Quick Summary/Log Line
Writing for Interactive Media is a comprehensive how-to guide that demystifies the complex process of interactive writing.

TARGET READERS

The section on target readers is where you answer a few key questions about your target audience such as:

- Who is the audience? (demographic information)
- What are their buying habits?
- What's the primary reason that somebody would purchase this book?

The following is an example of this section taken from Wimberley and Samsel's book proposal:

Target Readers
This book is targeted at writers, graphic designers, business communication specialists, computer programmers, feature film screenwriters, multimedia producers, technology professionals, academia, and students of new media.

The target audience is well educated and regularly purchases books and similar materials for research and educational purposes.

This book is a comprehensive resource that provides step-by-step instructions on how to write interactive media applications, from idea to finished product.

CONCEPT OVERVIEW

Most nonfiction proposals start with an overview of the basic concept. This is a summary of the idea and tells how the book is different from the other 60,000 books now being published each year.

Concept Overview
Want to write an interactive CD-ROM game? How about an online cybersoap or a multimedia sales and training application?

Following the *Interactive Writer's Handbook* comes the second in a series begun by authors Jon Samsel and Darryl Wimberley that examines the daily evolving arena of interactive storytelling.

Expanding on the concerns of the first book, which compared television and filmed narratives with their classic analogs in the interactive arena, this new title, *Writing for Interactive Media*, examines the entire gamut of multimedia activity, from Internet murder mysteries to educational kiosks, from Web-based training to ongoing experiments that take gaming narratives from the living room to players across the globe.

Building on the notion of closed and open story systems, the authors map specific requirements and unique methodologies tailored for the interactive environment that prospective writers want to master. The book is a toolbox and a theoretical construct, useful to writers and academics seeking to exploit or make sense out of the whole array of interactive environments.

THE KEY FEATURES AND SELLING POINTS OF THE BOOK

Editors like book proposals that clearly highlight the best features the book has to offer, especially those elements that will help their marketing and sales team push large quantities of your book into the marketplace. Without clear direction in this area, an author is asking the busy editor (and staff) to think too hard. Your book proposal should not leave anything to chance. Identify the book's best features and its competitive advantages.

Oftentimes, the author's insights in this area are incorporated into the back cover copy of the book, should the publisher decide to publish the book. And why not? Who else knows the book's content better than the author?

Wimberley and Samsel identified numerous features that would help convince a publisher that their manuscript was worthy of publication.

Key Features and Selling Points of the Book
- The number of writers looking to expand their careers into new media production and the Internet will be in the hundreds of thousands in the next few years.
- Writers seeking assistance on writing, design, and legal issues will look to resources such as books in greater numbers than ever before.

- Few other books provide in-depth exploration of the creative issues crucial to interactive writing. The market is ripe.
- The authors previously wrote the *Interactive Writer's Handbook,* the *first book of its kind* to explore the complex subject of interactive writing. The book was adopted as a textbook by the following colleges, trade schools, and universities:

  George Washington University
  UCLA
  San Francisco State University
  Duquesne University
  Johns Hopkins University
  University of Massachusetts
  Loyola Marymount University, Los Angeles
  UC Irvine
  Florida State University
  Boston University
  Lange Community College
  Ball State University
  Simi Valley Adult School
  Southern Illinois University
  Long Beach State University
  Masters Institute
  Santa Barbara City College
  University of Oregon
  U.S. International University, San Diego
  California Lutheran University
  University of Advancing Computer Technology
  Wayne State University
  Collin County Community College

- The authors are noted authorities in the craft of writing. Both have university-level teaching experience in the subjects of screenwriting and interactive writing. Samsel has lectured at numerous computer and film-related events worldwide. Both are published authors and produced screenwriters.

- The book deconstructs actual interactive multimedia projects that have been produced and poses insightful questions to some of the leading writers, agents, and attorneys working in the field.

AUTHOR'S CREDENTIALS/QUALIFICATIONS

If you are an authority on the subject, or have special credentials for doing a book on it, state these facts up front. Mention any previously published books and toot your own horn if your track record includes any bestsellers. Don't be modest here, because this part of the proposal can elicit a positive editorial decision to sign your book. If you have no previous credits, then indicate any other published work you have done, including articles, short stories, newspaper work, and columns.

Author Bios

Jon Samsel is a senior consultant with Cognitiative, a San Francisco–based market research and consulting company servicing the technology industry.

Samsel wrote and produced *The Killer Content Workbook: An Interactive Guide for Exploring Creativity, Creative Development and Business Development Issues for the Interactive Media Developer*. He also wrote and/or edited ten electronic books/papers including *Silicon Valley to Hollywood: Top Ten Trends in Multi-Player Games and Online Entertainment*, *Going Global: Multimedia Marketing and Distribution*, the *Interactive Music Handbook*, and the *Interactive Writer's Handbook*. Samsel is also the co-author of two books published by Allworth Press: *Writing for Interactive Media: The Complete Guide* and *How to Write Articles That Sell*.

Mr. Samsel holds a B.A. in communications from California State University, Fullerton. He is an adjunct instructor in Web writing and design at UCLA Extension. He created Orange County's first university-level writing course for interactive media at UC Irvine and currently teaches Writing the Nonfiction Book Proposal and Writing for Interactive Multimedia.

Darryl Wimberley, Ph.D., is an author, novelist, and screen-writer residing in Austin, Texas. Wimberley has had over ten feature film screenplays optioned since 1980 and two produced feature credits. Currently, he has a two-book writing deal with St. Martin's Press. Wimberley has a broad educational background, with a major in international affairs and a minor in engineering sciences from the U.S. Air Force Academy, a master's degree in literature from St. Mary's University in San Antonio, Texas, and a doctorate in film theory and criticism from the University of Texas at Austin.

TABLE OF CONTENTS

The table of contents highlights the contents the authors plan to cover in the book. A thorough and complete table of contents allows editors to ease into the core ideas of the book without overwhelming them with detail. Tables of contents come in two formats: (1) bullet point and (2) prose. Either one or both can be used.

Table of Contents (Bullet Point)

Part I. Form and Function
  1. Skills You'll Need
  2. Structure out of Chaos
  3. What Interactive Documents Look Like

Part II. Interactivity and Narrative
  4. Homer to Cyberbard, What's the Difference?
  5. Immersion and the Seamless Experience
  6. What's Writing Got to Do with It?
  7. Story: Theory and Practice
  8. What Is an Interactive Story?
  9. God, Three Acts, and the Spine
  10. Performing Character
  11. Toward an Interactive Aesthetic
  12. Conversations with Kaplan, Stephenson, and Roach

Part III. Hybrids and Hypertext

Part IV. Informational Multimedia

Part V. Frequently Asked Questions about Writing for Interactive Media

Table of Contents (Prose)

Until now, there have been precious few resources for interactive writers and designers. With that in mind, the "best creative practices" of those artists on the front lines of the digital revolution will be examined in this book to provide some guidance and insight into the emerging field of interactive writing.

The first section of this five-part book introduces the key skills and concepts every interactive writer needs to know in order to be cyberliterate, such as how to plan and structure your interactive ideas, create dynamic flowcharts, and how to organize the written document.

In part two we'll take a look at what all good stories have in common. We'll look hard at what makes interactive texts different from novels, films, and television, and see what those differences mean for the interactive writer. We'll talk about immersion and the seamless experience. We'll discuss how the three-act structure fits into interactive narrative. And we'll also take a look at how to develop characters for interactive dramas and gather around the campfire for conversations with some of today's most celebrated "story-artists."

Part three takes us away from narrative as we delve into hypertext fiction and the World Wide Web. We'll deconstruct MGM's online rock-and-roll murder mystery, *Paul Is Dead*, and reconstruct the role-playing saga known as *Myst*.

Part four explores the art of informational multimedia. Topics of interest include corporate uses of interactive multimedia, interactive education, and CD-ROM tutorials. We'll show writers how to implement instructional methodology into their concept documents. We'll also talk about how writers can build more productive and engaging Web sites.

Finally, part five tackles frequently asked questions concerning writers of all skill levels. Topics include the importance of networking, advice on deal-making, tips on creativity, dealing with rejection, how best to follow up submissions, and common mistakes to avoid when writing interactive documents.

We live in an exciting age where the story and the teller are merging in a garden of forking paths. The audience is no longer a passive but an active participant in all that interactivity has to offer. New methods of communication and expression must be forged. And more and more it is the writer—the electronic scribe of the information age—who leads the charge.

COMPETITION

Editors rarely buy a book after reading a proposal without a clear understanding of those books that are similar and closest to yours. Here is your opportunity to compare your book with the strongest competing ones.

Does your book cover more, read better, offer newer and more helpful information? You need to point out clearly how your book is superior to others on the subject. Perhaps your book meets the needs of readers more effectively. Your must-look-at reference tool for this competition and comparison report is *Books in Print*. You will find a copy of this tool in most large libraries. You can also visit one of the online bookstores such as Amazon.com, Inc. (*www.amazon.com*), Barnes and Noble (*www.barnesandnoble.com*), Books Now (*www.booksnow.com*), Book Stacks (*www.bookstacks.com*), or netMarket's Book.com (*www.net-*

market.com). Most of these Web sites have excellent search engines that allow you to look up a book topic, find all titles in print that relate to your subject, and provide you with vital information on the title such as the ISBN, the publisher's name, the author's name, date published, and a book summary.

Never send a proposal that omits highlighting the competition; it has become a required element for all nonfiction proposals. A book proposal about business and the Internet might highlight the competition as follows: *The Net Zone* belongs in the emerging new category of business books that address information technology, organizational processes, and business theory as they pertain to and impact the new economy. In terms of style, *The Net Zone* most closely resembles *Crossing the Chasm* by Geoffrey Moore and *Net Gain* by John Hagel and Arthur G. Armstrong—for the way each combines honest and straightforward advice, business theory and real-life case studies. There are only a handful of related business titles that address some of the Internet business issues that are explored in *The Net Zone*, namely: *Blur: The Speed of Change in the Connected Economy*, by Christopher Meyer and Stan Davis. This is a well-crafted book focusing on the speed of change in a connected economy—where advantage is temporary and nothing is fixed in space or time. This is a compassionate guide with lots of useful and inspiring stories. *The Net Zone* is different in that it takes a focused, strategic look at the Web issues confronting corporate management. *The Digital Economy: Promise and Peril in the Age of Networked Intelligence*, by Don Tapscott. This book delves deeply into the impact of the digital revolution on society. There are some good chapters which tackle business transformation models and leadership skills—topics we will cover in *The Net Zone*, but with a slightly different approach. Tapscott's case studies are informative, but are beginning to feel a bit dated. *The Net Zone* is different in that it focuses exclusively on the Web and its impact on business, rather than the broader issue of technology's impact on economic systems.

CHAPTER SUMMARY

The last major element in a proposal lineup is the chapter summary. Here you will write one or two brief paragraphs that summarize each chapter of your book. This is the place in a proposal where an author can shine and show a keen grasp of the subject. This proposal section goes a long way in convincing an editor that you know your subject well, have thought it out, done your research and interviews, and captured your vision of the book on paper.

Length of Your Proposal

Most book proposals run about twenty pages, but the length can vary from only a few pages to fifty or more. The idea is to show a plan for the book, not to make a book out of the proposal. Length seems to depend on the particular author and the type of book involved.

As a general rule, don't let your proposals run too long. Authors have been known to exhaust themselves on a proposal when it's the book that deserves the bulk of their attention. Don't wear yourself out on the proposal to the point where you have little or no energy left for the book.

Many authors also state an estimated length for the book and when it will be delivered to the publisher. Be sure to allow enough extra time to complete a book because life has a way of presenting delays. Give yourself more time to complete a manuscript than you believe is necessary. This extra time may come in handy and will serve as a cushion and insurance that you will meet your manuscript deadline.

Check your proposal carefully for spelling errors and any others errors you can spot. Errors like misspelled words will cause an editor to stop reading your proposal and to reach instead for a fresh one that is or looks more professional. This sounds like a little step, but many writers ignore it and send in proposals and manuscripts with lots of errors. Don't cut your proposal off at the pass. Make certain it is error free with all words spelled correctly. You'll be glad you checked and corrected it.

Strive to be a professional at every step of the author-editor-publisher (and/or agent) process. You will sell more books and be more proud of them when they are published. Have pride in each book you do. Make it your best effort for that book at that time.

A Well-Written Book Proposal Serves as a Business Proposition

A well-done proposal acts as a signal to an editor that the project should receive careful attention. Proposals that receive a quick response usually receive a negative response. Errors or poor writing tip off the editor that the project is not of the quality he or she is seeking. Proposals that are well executed, and on subjects that fit a publisher's list, take longer for a decision. Obviously, some proposals arrive at the right time, are on target, and excite an editor's enthusiasm. Such proposals are a delight to editors (and may also receive a quick response).

Try your best to send only terrific proposals to publishers. They take more time and effort, but the positive results they can bring are worth it. It also takes time, sometimes a lot of it, to complete a top-notch proposal for a book.

Why Many Authors Dislike Proposals and Outlines

Different authors give various reasons why they dislike doing outlines and proposals. Here are the general reasons they turn thumbs down on one or both:

1. Outlines set a limit on the creative process. The author may feel that he or she cannot make any changes once the outline has been set.
2. The minds of many authors go blank when they have to do an outline.
3. Changes are quite likely to suggest themselves to an author while the actual writing is being done.
4. "Outlines are flat and cold," say a number of authors.
5. An outline, even a proposal, may be a poor indicator of the final book. The completed book may turn out far better than the proposal or outline suggested. An outline or proposal may not give an accurate appraisal of the book's potential, style, and quality of writing; or may even be misleading in a number of ways. Yet editors may turn the project down if they don't like the way the proposal or outline reads.

6. When it comes to fiction, many novelists prefer to "turn a character loose" and see what happens. They like to discover the story as they write it, and an outline or synopsis cramps this method.
7. Many authors are often more stimulated by working from an opening sentence or setting and don't like feeling restricted by what was stated in an outline or proposal.
8. Some authors swear that a proposal or outline simply short-circuits their enthusiasm for a project.

The final decision is up to the author. Here is a method that has worked well for many authors: if your book is a novel, do not use an outline; if your book is nonfiction, use an outline or proposal. In any case, to sell a nonfiction book these days, you will usually have to complete a proposal first.

In fiction, it naturally helps to know your main characters when beginning a novel, along with an idea for the setting and ending. Some planning is probably a must for a novel (for most authors), and that will mean a carefully thought-out synopsis.

Remember that a promising proposal for a nonfiction book can go a long way toward selling your project to an editor. Unless novels are your specialty, sound outlines and proposals for nonfiction books will likely mean more book contracts for you.

Discover what works best for you through experience. Keep in mind that you can always tear up an outline, even a proposal, change it to please you, or do a brand new one.

The point is to put your best foot forward—in hopes that the end result is a book with your name on it.

—==◆==—

CHAPTER 11

The Deal: What It Takes to Land an Elusive Publishing Contract

Authors sometimes voice their frustration in trying to find the right publisher for their manuscripts. Even experienced authors with track records are sometimes uncertain which publisher is right for certain books. Darryl Wimberley offers this blunt advice for writers looking to land a publishing contract: "If you're a writer, you need to hunt with a shotgun, not a rifle."

How to Find the Right Publisher

One of the best ways to get a handle on this quest is to request the latest catalogs from the publishers you are considering. After studying them, pick the companies you believe would do the best job on your type of book. Be sure your choices are those publishers actually doing that type of book. Checking their list will reveal that information to you.

Many authors find the right publisher via an agent. A key reason authors sign with agents is that any agent worth his or her salt knows which publisher is best for a given book. Agents are close to the business and deal with all the major publishers, so they become good at matching books with publishers.

Another possible way to find the right publisher is expensive, but it has worked for a number of authors. You simply pack your bags and visit New York City, where most of the top publishers are located. You visit different publishing offices in hopes of getting a lead on the right one for your book. It's best to write them before arriving in New York to save your time. Some will not see you, but others may be willing to see what you have, providing you have written specific editors first and requested an appointment.

Editors are so pressed for time these days that this last method—the trip to New York—could fail completely. The test will be to write editors first and see if any reply and actually grant you an appointment. If you can land meetings with at least two editors, take a trip to the Big Apple and see what happens. You never know till you try.

How to Evaluate a Publishing Company

Studying a publisher's catalog will give you a feel for the type of books they seem to like. Visiting a publisher's office can also help you evaluate them. Most publishers display their current books in their lobby areas near the receptionist. In some publishing offices, you will get a cold, unresponsive reaction. Others are completely polite and professional.

You are more likely to be treated kindly and courteously by publishers than by some of the powerhouse agents. Some of these hotshot agents are prima donnas and won't give you the time of day unless you're a big-time, meganame author. Again, if you plan to contact agents, too, while visiting New York, be sure to write them first for an appointment. If any agree to see you, consider yourself fortunate.

One of the biggest mistakes new authors make is to send novels to publishers who don't want fiction or nonfiction proposals to publishers mainly interested in novels. Basically, it's never a good idea to send unsolicited material to any publisher. Only send what you are *asked* to send. Query the publishers first, or call and ask for their manuscript submission guidelines. You might ask if you can speak to an editor to find out if he or she is interested in seeing a proposal for your book. Follow this simple rule and you will save time, money, and much aggravation.

Reading the trade journals of publishing can give you clues about different publishers, and that will help you to evaluate them. Going online and visiting the Web sites of various publishing houses is also a great way to get to know a publisher. You can learn about their corporate policies, key officers and/or editors, submission policies, front list titles, back list titles, and almost anything you need to know about them. Best of all, you can access this information twenty-four hours a day at your convenience.

The Submission Process

Perhaps a better phrase for the submission process is "the numbers game." Practically all publishers these days state flat out that they absolutely want to be queried first. The numbers game is thus played with queries, proposals, or a partial to complete manuscript. Some authors claim they got a go-ahead from at least a few publishers after sending twenty query letters. But your results may vary from quite a few positive responses to none. This might improve somewhat by offering to send a proposal, but there is no assurance of this.

Author Aliske Webb tried to place her novel with 150 publishers and was rejected by all of them. Still, she refused to give up. "We went the usual route, sending the book to all 150 publishers." Rejected but still game, Webb and her husband sold their home, self-published the book, *Twelve Golden Threads: Lessons for Successful Living from Grama's Quilt,* and made a tour of quilt shows all over America. Some two and one-half years later and 25,000 copies sold, Webb signed with a small publisher in Pennsylvania. By this time, some major publishers in New York finally realized the large untapped market for Webb's book. She was soon offered a four-book contract for a substantial amount.

Author Darryl Wimberley offers his thoughts on submitting manuscripts: "You have to submit every place, all the time. Keep track of your submissions and never stop! Because you cannot know in advance which avenue, if any, will get your book placed."

An author's determination and faith in his or her work can make all the difference in success or failure. You should always live with the hope that one day you will hit it big. Give up, on the other hand, and you're down for the count.

Queries and Cover Letters

Should you query a publisher first to see if your idea is of interest? Since most editors have little or no spare time, a strong case can be made for first sending a query letter regarding your idea. Editors appreciate this consideration and will be able to get back to you faster because of it. The query letter has grown considerably in importance in recent years. Many editors of books, magazines, and newspapers list a preliminary query letter as a definite requirement for doing business with them.

The advantage of the query letter is that it allows you to sell your book before it's even written. It hits the editor with your basic book idea, and if the editor likes the sound of it, he or she will probably want to see more.

A query also gives the editor an idea of your writing style, shows the range of your thoughts about the subject of the book, and provides hints as to whether your basic idea and choice of subject indicate a worthwhile project. A good query letter can convince an editor that you have what it takes to complete a book.

It makes sense to find out if an editor is receptive to your book idea. Most publishers develop a certain kind of book list over the years. A cookbook, for example, or a title on investing, or any number of other subjects may be completely wrong for a given publisher.

The author saves time, and so does the editor, when you first send a query letter. You'd be surprised how many would-be authors send their manuscripts to publishers with no knowledge of what a particular company specializes in. Computer books shouldn't be sent to a publisher that exclusively produces detective novels. Religious books sometimes arrive in the offices of a craft or gardening publisher.

A one-page letter (typed and single-spaced) should be enough to describe your book idea, explain why you are an expert on the subject, and why you believe the title would perform well in the market.

The longer the query, the less likely it is to be read. A long letter—more than two pages—is guaranteed to take longer to be read and answered. It's what you say, and the promising quality of your idea, that count the most.

A go-ahead response to a query letter is no guarantee of acceptance, but it does usually signal an editor's interest in your idea and possible desire to see an outline and a few sample chapters.

A cover letter is usually enclosed along with the manuscript you are submitting. A cover letter should be brief—a half page to one page—that summarizes the manuscript, gives a word count, a brief overview of your writing history/qualifications, and a request that the editor consider the manuscript for publication.

It's good etiquette and standard procedure to include a self-addressed, stamped envelope (SASE) with anything you send to an editor or publisher—especially if you expect a timely reply. Failure to include one with your submission sometimes signals that the writer is an amateur. On the other hand, it can be argued that enclosing an SASE sometimes invites a rejection and may be judged amateurish by some editors. Can you imagine Hemingway or Mary Higgins Clark enclosing a return envelope with their work?

Hit Them with an Idea First

Let us assume that you have come up with a new book idea. You like it and believe it would sell. How do you present your idea to publishers? Here are some choices open to you:

1. Describe your idea *briefly* (a few paragraphs to a full page) and draft a standard query letter.
2. Send a query to a dozen publishers and offer to follow up with an outline and sample chapter. This is the *multiple submission* method. Numerous authors report good results from using it. You can send multiple query letters and also multiple outlines and chapters to a dozen or more publishers.
3. When you write or phone the editor, have a strong working title for your book. This can help keep the idea better fixed in the editor's mind.

4. Simply state that you want to write a book on a given subject and tell why you believe it might be right for that publisher. Do this for each company you contact.
5. Ask the editor if there is current interest in new book projects. Name the categories that include your book ideas, such as self-help, how-to, children's books, adventure novels, or romances. Most people in the industry think of romances, Westerns, and mysteries (as well as certain other types) as genre books.

This last method (number 5) is really just a request for an editor's okay to send some new book projects. It sometimes works if your timing is right. An editor may well be looking for new titles in certain categories, like health or popular psychology, for example, so you might get a green light to send what you have in those categories.

Good Idea, Wrong Publisher

This can and does happen to many authors. Even with lots of experience, some still find it difficult to remember which publishers do certain types of books. With so many book publishers in the United States alone, it can be quite a task to remember who wants what, but it is very important. If you send your novel to a nonfiction publisher, you've created work for them without increasing your chances of publishing the project. You've also made a poor impression on an editor who you may want to approach later about a non-fiction project.

A good way to handle matching a book idea with the right publisher is to request the latest catalogs from publishers you think might be interested in your project. Or, you can log on to the Internet and visit the publishers' Web sites. After studying them, pick the companies that seem like the best match for your book idea. A large percentage of rejections are the result of an author sending a proposal to the wrong publisher.

Try to send your new ideas and book projects to the *right* publishers. This matching will increase the likelihood of landing a contract.

Remember that the titles listed in a catalog may not be what an editor presently wants. Maybe the publisher has decided to change its line of books. Ask the editor if the books listed in the catalog are a good indication of what is wanted.

Slush-Pile Submissions

Some editors are willing to read projects sent in cold. Most major publishers receive thousands of submissions a year. When no name is on the submission—no specific editor to whom the material is addressed—it will go into the slush pile. Over time, the slush pile grows into quite a lot of projects for consideration. Editors who are willing to take a look at such submissions do so as their time allows. Some editors will not read slush-pile material. Some publishing houses will not even accept unsolicited manuscripts.

It is far wiser for an author to send material to a specific editor. Then, on its arrival, the submission will be routed to a living human being, which is much better than being thrown in the slush pile.

At publishing houses that do accept unsolicited manuscripts, slush-pile submissions go through the following process. Their dates of arrival are logged in along with the names and addresses of the authors. Editorial assistants usually read them first. The screened manuscripts are sorted into categories, indicating which deserve more attention, which show the author has talent (even though the manuscript is not good enough), and which must be returned as definitely unsuitable. Slush-pile submissions deemed worthy of more time and discussion may be held for several months so each project can receive the proper attention.

So, if you send your manuscript unsolicited, be prepared for a long wait before you hear anything—and there's always the chance you may never have your manuscript returned. Ultimately, the slush-pile method is too risky. If you have a worthy manuscript, why waste time with it and run the risk of losing it? Write the editor a query letter first, describing your work and asking if the editor would be interested in seeing it.

How to Follow Up: Phone, Fax, E-mail, or Snail Mail?

Following up on submissions is tricky and involves tact and timing. A number of editors absolutely go ballistic if any author (less than a big name) phones them without prior permission. Other editors say they don't mind and will talk briefly on the phone if their schedule permits. Just be certain you know how a particular editor feels about it.

Fax is another way to touch base with an editor; but with the number of people in some publishing offices, one wonders if the editor you wish to reach will get the fax. Still, it's an excellent, rapid way to communicate, and more and more authors are using faxes.

E-mail is also a quick way to send an editor a message, and more and more authors are using it. It can be used to ask if the editor received your query letter, proposal, or even a partial manuscript. The editor can quickly respond by e-mail. The swiftness of this method makes it appealing, and an author can get a response much faster this way.

Snail mail is the usual standard letter route, which can take a week, sometimes longer, just for your communication to get to New York. There are editors who will respond to a standard letter, but the era of slow-paced mail is on the way out. Some editors may actually be influenced by the method an author uses today to communicate. Still, America is supposed to be a free country, and some authors choose to communicate this way. This will probably change in the early years of the twenty-first century as more authors switch to e-mail, fax, or the old telephone.

How to Negotiate a Writing Deal

Now that you have aroused the interest of a publisher enough to be offered a book deal, you need to establish clear and definitive parameters that are in your best interests. When the publisher and author come together (usually via telephone) to work out the fine print of a deal, the process is referred to as a negotiation. Both sides state what they want and expect from the other side, an agreement is reached, and the deal is done.

It's a good idea to have an experienced agent or attorney negotiate a deal on your behalf. Experienced negotiators can oftentimes get you more money and perks than you could have negotiated on your own. They also serve as a buffer between you and the publisher—so that the artist/publisher relationship never deteriorates over money conflicts. Obviously, any book deal should be written down, examined with a fine-tooth comb by your legal expert, and signed by all involved parties.

The following are some major issues authors should address during negotiations:

- Establish realistic development time schedules with some backup plans for delays.

- Establish realistic payment schedules.

- Set reasonable credit requirements (e.g., where your name will appear on the book).

- Set a realistic approval process (comment period) that doesn't delay development yet ensures a quality product.

- Establish reasonable boundaries for future content revisions (if necessary).

- Create a "drop-dead clause" (i.e., what happens if the publisher decides to terminate you from the project or terminate the project completely? Is the terminating party required to pay the other party some form of compensation?).

- Agree to "goodies clauses" (complimentary copies of the product, travel expenses, per diem, royalties).

- Provide for a resolution process in the event of disagreement (a mutually trusted third party or arbitrator).

Here are some general tips for improving the quality of your negotiations:

- Formulate an agenda in advance of negotiations (what you need versus what you'd like).

- Find some common ground with the person with whom you are negotiating. Does the person like sports? Does he or she have kids? Light conversation prior to negotiating allows each side to be more forthcoming.

- Never lie. Unethical behavior is rarely rewarded. If you must bend the truth, do it sparingly.

- Try not to negotiate your own deal. Tough negotiations can sometimes resemble a bitter divorce. It sours the client/artist relationship.

- Listen calmly to the publisher's requests and arguments. There will be plenty of time to present your counteroffer later.

- Never swear, be demanding, or hang up on the publisher (it only makes you look childish).

- Never concede a point unless you receive a comparable deal point in return. You must be willing to walk away from a deal if you are being forced to concede a point you are passionate about.

- Be careful what you ask for in a deal. You may actually get it!

- Take rigorous notes and follow up all meetings with a memo outlining all agreed-upon terms.

- Don't gossip about the points in the final deal or tell stories about the opposing negotiator. The opposing side will most surely remember your big mouth if you ever have to negotiate with them again.

At the conclusion of the deal, take your opponent to lunch or send over a gift basket. A simple act of kindness heals all egos.

The Book Publishing Contract

Book publishing contracts have become fairly standardized over the years. Thanks to computers, a publisher need only punch in a new set of facts and figures and a brand-new author-publisher agreement will spit out of the printer in a matter of minutes.

Allworth Press publishes a great book called *Business and Legal Forms for Authors and Self-Publishers*. It's a great resource for authors looking to learn more about the various "form contracts" used in the industry, including useful author agreements such as the book publishing contract reprinted below:

Book Publishing Contract
(COURTESY OF ALLWORTH PRESS)

Agreement, entered into as of this _____ day of _____, _____, between _____, located at _____ (hereinafter referred to as the "Publisher"), and _____, located at _____ (hereinafter referred to as the "Author").

Whereas, the Author wishes to create a book on the subject of _____ (hereinafter referred to as the "Work"),

Whereas, the Publisher is familiar with the authorship of the Author and wishes to distribute such a work, and

Whereas, the parties wish to have said distribution performed subject to the mutual obligations, covenants, and conditions herein.

Now, therefore, in consideration of the foregoing premises and the mutual covenants hereinafter set forth and other valuable considerations, the parties hereto agree as follows:

1. Grant of Rights. The Author grants, conveys, and transfers to the Publisher in that unpublished Work titled _____ _____ certain limited rights as follows:

(A) To publish the Work in the form of a _____ book,
(B) In the territory of _____,
(C) In the _____ language, and
(D) For a term of _____ years.

2. Reservation and Reversion of Rights. All rights not specifically granted to the Publisher are reserved to the Author, including but not limited to electronic rights, which are defined as rights in the digitized form of works that can be encoded, stored, and retrieved from such media as computer disks, CD-ROMs, computer databases, and network servers.

3. Delivery of Manuscript. On or before the _____ day of _____, _____, the Author shall deliver to the Publisher a complete manuscript of approximately _____ words, which shall be reasonably satisfactory in form and content to the Publisher and in conformity with any outline or description attached hereto and made part hereof. The manuscript shall be in the following form: ☐ double-spaced hard copy ☐ computer files (specify format _____). The manuscript shall include the additional materials listed in Paragraph 4 (except that if an index is to be provided by the Author, it shall be delivered to the Publisher within thirty (30) days of Author's receipt of paginated galleys). If the Author fails to deliver the complete manuscript within ninety (90) days after receiving notice from the Publisher of failure to deliver on time, the Publisher shall have the right to terminate this Agreement and receive back from the Author all monies advanced to the Author pursuant to Paragraphs 4, 5, and 9. If the Author delivers a manuscript which, after being given detailed instructions for revisions by the Publisher and _____ days to complete such revisions, is not reasonably acceptable to the Publisher, then monies advanced to the Author pursuant to Paragraphs 4, 5, and 9 shall be ☐ retained by the Author ☐ repaid to the Publisher ☐ repaid to the Publisher only in the event the Author subsequently signs a contract with another Publisher for the Work.

4. Additional Materials. The following materials shall be provided by the Author: _____
_____

The cost of providing these additional materials shall be borne by the Author, provided, however, that the Publisher at the time of signing this Agreement shall give a nonrefundable payment of $_____

to assist the Author in defraying these costs, which payment shall not be deemed an advance to the Author and shall not be recouped as such.

5. Permissions. The Author agrees to obtain all permissions that are necessary for the use of materials copyrighted by others. The cost of providing these permissions shall be borne by the Author, provided, however, that the Publisher at the time of signing this Agreement shall give a nonrefundable payment of $_____ to assist the Author in defraying these costs, which payment shall not be deemed an advance to the Author and shall not be recouped as such. Permissions shall be obtained in writing and copies shall be provided to the Publisher when the manuscript is delivered.

6. Duty to Publish. The Publisher shall publish the Work within _____ months of the delivery of the complete manuscript. Failure to so publish shall give the Author the right to terminate this Agreement ninety (90) days after giving written notice to the Publisher of the failure to make timely publication. In the event of such termination, the Author shall have no obligation to return monies received pursuant to Paragraphs 4, 5, and 9.

7. Royalties. The Publisher shall pay the Author the following royalties: _____ percent of the suggested retail price on the first 5,000 copies sold, _____ percent of the suggested retail price on the next 5,000 copies sold, and _____ percent of the suggested retail price on all copies sold thereafter.

These royalty rates shall be discounted only in the following circumstances: _____
_____

All copies sold shall be cumulated for purposes of escalations in the royalty rates, including revised editions, except for editions in a different form (such as a paperback reprint of a hardcover original), which shall be cumulated separately. Copies sold shall be reduced by copies returned in the same royalty category in which the copies were originally reported as sold.

In the event the Publisher has the right pursuant to Paragraph 1(A) to publish the Work in more than one form, the royalty rates specified above shall apply to publication in the form of a _____ book and the royalty rates for other forms shall be specified here:

_____

_____

_____

8. Subsidiary Rights. The following subsidiary rights may be licensed by the party indicated and the proceeds divided as specified herein:

Subsidiary Right	Right to License		Division of Proceeds	
	Author	Publisher	Author	Publisher
_____	_____	_____	_____	_____
_____	_____	_____	_____	_____
_____	_____	_____	_____	_____
_____	_____	_____	_____	_____
_____	_____	_____	_____	_____
_____	_____	_____	_____	_____

If the division of proceeds for any subsidiary right changes after the sale of a certain number of copies, indicate which right, the number of copies required to be sold, and the new division of proceeds:

_____

_____

_____

The right to license any subsidiary right not set forth in this Paragraph is retained by the Author.

Licensing income shall be divided as specified herein without any reductions for expenses of any kind. Licensing income shall be collected by the party authorized to license the right and the appropriate percentage remitted by that party to the other party within ten (10) days of receipt. Copies of all licenses shall be provided to both parties immediately upon receipt.

9. Advances. The Publisher shall, at the time of signing this Agreement, pay to the Author a nonrefundable advance of $_____, which advance shall be recouped by the Publisher from payments due to the Author pursuant to Paragraph 11 of this Agreement.

10. Accountings. Commencing as of the date of publication, the Publisher shall report every _____ months to the Author, showing for that period and cumulatively to date the number of copies printed and bound, the number of copies sold and returned for each royalty rate, the number of copies distributed free for publicity purposes, the number of copies remaindered, destroyed, or lost, and the royalties paid to and owed to the Author. If the Publisher sets up a reserve against returns of books, the reserve may only be set up for the four accounting periods following the first publication of the Work and shall in no event exceed 15 percent of royalties due to the Author in any period.

11. Payments. The Publisher shall pay the Author all monies due Author pursuant to Paragraph 10 within thirty (30) days of the close of each accounting period.

12. Right of Inspection. The Author shall, upon the giving of written notice, have the right to inspect the Publisher's books of account to verify the accountings. If errors in any such accounting are found to be to the Author's disadvantage and represent more than 5 percent of the payment to the Author pursuant to the said accounting, the cost of inspection shall be paid by the Publisher.

13. Copyright and Authorship Credit. The Publisher shall, as an express condition of receiving the grant of rights specified in Paragraph 1, take the necessary steps to register the copyright on behalf of the Author and in the Author's name and shall place copyright notice in the Author's name on all copies of the Work. The Author shall receive authorship credit as follows: _____

14. Warranty and Indemnity. The Author warrants and represents that he or she is the sole creator of the Work and owns all rights granted under this Agreement, that the Work is an original creation and has not previously been published (indicate any parts that have been previously published), that the Work does not infringe any other person's copyrights or rights of literary property, nor, to his or her knowledge, does it violate the rights of privacy of, or libel, other persons. The Author agrees to indemnify the Publisher against any final judgment for damages (after all appeals have been exhausted) in any lawsuit based on an actual breach of the foregoing warranties. In addition, the Author shall pay the Publisher's reasonable costs and attorney's fees incurred in defending such a lawsuit, unless the Author chooses to retain his or her own attorney to defend such lawsuit. The Author makes no warranties and shall have no obligation to indemnify the Publisher with respect to materials inserted in the Work at the Publisher's request. Notwithstanding any of the foregoing, in no event shall the Author's liability under this Paragraph exceed $_____ or _____ percent of sums payable to the Author under this Agreement, whichever is the lesser. In the event a lawsuit is brought that may result in the Author having breached his or her warranties under this Paragraph, the Publisher shall have the right to withhold and place in an escrow account _____ percent of sums payable to the Author pursuant to Paragraph 11, but in no event may said withholding exceed the damages alleged in the complaint.

15. Artistic Control. The Author and Publisher shall consult with one another with respect to the title of the Work, the price of the Work, the method and means of advertising and selling the Work, the number and destination of free copies, the number of copies to be printed, the method of printing and other publishing processes, the exact date of publication, the form, style, size, type, paper to be used, and like details, how long the plates or type shall be preserved and when they shall be destroyed and when new printings of the Work shall be made. In the event of disagreement after consultation, the Publisher shall have final power of decision over all the foregoing matters except the following, which shall be controlled by the Author:_____.

No changes shall be made in the complete manuscript of the Work by persons other than the Author, except for reasonable copyediting, unless the Author consents to such changes. Publisher shall provide the Author with galleys and proofs which the Author shall review and return to the Publisher within thirty (30) days of receipt. If the cost of the Author's alterations (other than for typesetting errors or unavoidable updating) exceeds _____ percent of the cost of the typography, the Publisher shall have the right to deduct such excess from royalties due Author hereunder.

16. Original Materials. Within thirty (30) days after publication, the Publisher shall return the original manuscript and all additional materials to the Author. The Publisher shall provide the Author with a copy of the page proofs, if the Author requests them prior to the date of publication.

17. Free Copies. The Author shall receive ten (10) free copies of the Work as published, after which the Author shall have the right to purchase additional copies at a _____ percent discount from the retail price.

18. Revisions. The Author agrees to revise the Work on request by the Publisher. If the Author cannot revise the Work or refuses to do so absent good cause, the Publisher shall have the right to have the Work revised by a person competent to do so and shall charge the costs of said revision against payments due the Author under Paragraph 11 for such revised edition.

19. Successors and Assigns. This Agreement may not be assigned by either party without the written consent of the other party hereto. The Author, however, shall retain the right to assign payments due hereunder without obtaining the Publisher's consent. This Agreement shall be binding on the parties and their respective heirs, administrators, successors, and assigns.

20. Infringement. In the event of an infringement of the rights granted under this Agreement to the Publisher, the Publisher and the

Author shall have the right to sue jointly for the infringement and, after deducting the expenses of bringing suit, to share equally in any recovery. If either party chooses not to join in the suit, the other party may proceed and, after deducting all the expenses of bringing the suit, any recovery shall be shared equally between the parties.

21. Termination. The Author shall have the right to terminate this Agreement by written notice if: (1) the Work goes out-of-print and the Publisher, within ninety (90) days of receiving notice from the Author that the Work is out-of-print, does not place the Work in print again (out-of-print shall mean that the Work is not available for sale in normal trade channels); (2) the Publisher fails to provide statements of account pursuant to Paragraph 10; (3) the Publisher fails to make payments pursuant to Paragraphs 4, 5, 9, or 11; or (4) the Publisher fails to publish in a timely manner pursuant to Paragraph 6. The Publisher shall have the right to terminate this Agreement as provided in Paragraph 3. This Agreement shall automatically terminate in the event of the Publisher's insolvency, bankruptcy, or assignment of assets for the benefit of creditors. In the event of termination of the Agreement, the Publisher shall grant, convey, and transfer all rights in the Work back to the Author.

22. Production Materials and Unbound Copies. Upon any termination, the Author may, within sixty (60) days of notification of such termination, purchase the plates, offset negatives, or computer drive tapes (if any) at their scrap value and any remaining copies at the lesser of cost or remainder value.

23. Promotion. The Author consents to the use of his or her name, portrait, or picture in connection with the promotion and advertising of the Work, provided such use is dignified and consistent with the Author's reputation.

24. Arbitration. All disputes arising under this Agreement shall be submitted to binding arbitration before _____ in the following location _____ and shall be settled in accordance with the rules of the American Arbitration

Association. Judgment upon the arbitration award may be entered in any court having jurisdiction thereof.

25. Notice. Where written notice is required hereunder, it may be given by use of first-class mail addressed to the Author or Publisher at the addresses given at the beginning of this Agreement and shall be deemed received five (5) days after mailing. Said addresses for notice may be changed by giving written notice of any new address to the other party.

26. Modifications in Writing. All modifications of this Agreement must be in writing and signed by both parties.

27. Waivers and Defaults. Any waiver of a breach or default hereunder shall not be deemed a waiver of a subsequent breach or default of either the same provision or any other provision of this Agreement.

28. Governing Law. This Agreement shall be governed by the laws of _____ State.

_____   _____
            Author   Publisher

                           By: _____
_____
Social Security Number   Authorized Signatory, Title

Author Income: Advances, Royalties, and Ancillary Rights

There are several ways you can build a second income from the books you write and place with publishers. Advances and royalties add to your yearly total as an author. There are also subsidiary rights sales (also called ancillary rights sales) to magazines, newspapers, book clubs, audiobook companies, and/or film companies. Other subsidiary rights include electronic rights, speaking engagements, and foreign rights fees. All these fees can add up to a hefty sum, assuming your book carves a respectable place for itself in the marketplace.

An advance is not a handout from a publisher to an author; it's your own money you receive on the future earnings (royalties) of your book. An advance means just that—an advance against the royalties to be earned by your book. When your book is published and selling, you won't get any more money until it has earned back the amount paid as an advance. So the publisher gets back the money advanced to an author when the book starts to sell. Many books, unfortunately, never earn back their advances. A number of others just break even. What every author shoots for, and publishers, too, are books that earn back their advances and then go on to earn a profitable return (or much better).

Prospective authors should realize that an advance can help you financially while you complete your manuscript. Many small publishers do not offer advances, but the major companies work this way, with half the advance paid when you sign a contract and the balance paid when a completed, and acceptable, manuscript is delivered to the publisher.

Once the book is published and selling, an author will receive royalty reports twice a year with any amount due enclosed. Most publishers send these royalty statements in the spring and fall along with any subsidiary rights payments.

Agent Margot Maley explains: "Writers can make a lot of money on ancillary deals. I have a few authors who make more money on speaking engagements relating to their books than they do on the books. Film and audio rights can be huge if you have the right book. Foreign rights can bring in as much or more income as the original English rights deal. CD-ROM rights have become less of a factor in the past few years and electronic rights, though still kept by most publishers, are not exercised all that often."

CHAPTER 12

Self-Publishing: Is It for You?

The truth about self-publishing is that it can go either way for an author. Some authors have lost most or all of their money on such projects. Others have regained their investments and a profit. Still others have done incredibly well with their self-published books usually after considerable effort, promotion, and personal selling.

Benefits of Self-Publishing

The idea of self-publishing is that just about anyone with a strong book idea can publish their own manuscript, provided there is money available to do so.

The number of small author-publisher companies has increased, and many of these one-person operations are thriving. If their books take off in the marketplace, these self-publishers keep the lion's share of the profits. Not having to split the profits is a big plus, but the other side of the coin is that self-publishers must bear all the expenses of producing, printing, and promoting the book. In a standard contract with a recognized publisher, the author is low man or woman on the totem pole. The publisher makes the most with the author getting a royalty percentage. But the recognized publisher pays for publishing the book, so self-publishing, despite these benefits, is a mixed bag.

For some authors, self-publishing may be easier than dealing with a known publisher. Some authors want, and seem to enjoy, doing it all—writing, producing, printing, selling, and promoting the book. Here are a few more benefits of self-publishing:

- Authors have greater control over their work

- There is a higher possible return on investment from self pub-lishing than from publishing with a third party

- It increases personal satisfaction and can be an ego booster

- Success is limited only by an author's tenacity and hard work

There is also little doubt that self-publishers will let their books die on the vine, as some large national publishers do, often because they must move on to other newer books on their lists.

The Risks of Self-Publishing

Every book is a lead book for a self-publisher, who sinks a lot of money, time, effort, and sometimes real sacrifice into the book. If the gamble pays off, the self-publisher makes a bundle when a major pub-lisher will offer to take over the small self-publisher's book.

Self-publishing is certainly a way to get the attention of the big publishers. If your book or books take off and chalk up a lot of sales, or bestsellers, the major publishers will sit up and take notice and contact you. Cliché or not, nothing succeeds like success, in this business as in others. This is especially true in today's era of the "blockbuster mentality," so rampant among major publishers.

Some major risks to self-publishing are as follows:

- It's a slow-growth/low-margin business opportunity

- Success is linked to amortizing hard costs and releasing multi-ple book titles over time

- Self-publishing has an "amateur" stigma attached to it

- There are a lot of small publishers competing for recognition and awareness

- Many small publishers are underfinanced and cannot survive during slow sales periods or radical shifts in the marketplace

Another risk to self-publishers is the large wholesale order. While a self-publisher's initial reaction to a large order of 5,000–10,000 books may be joy, the reality is that this large order may lead a self-publisher down the path to bankruptcy! Many self-publishers will finance a large volume of books to be put to press, then wait six to twelve months for a check from the wholesaler. Assuming they can survive that long, given the fact that they may be $15,000–$30,000 in debt, a wholesaler may later come back with significant returns and ask for some of its money back. Many small presses and self-publishers have gone under this way. Prove that as a self-publisher you can deliver the goods with strong-selling books, meaning bestsellers, and you may not have to stay a self-publisher unless that is your wish.

The sales for a book in the first year are critical and usually determine what its fate will be when controlled by a large national publisher. It may die a quick death by, or before, the end of the first year. For a self-publisher, it's different. The first year is used to build a solid market for a future of sustained sales. A large New York publisher may sell only five thousand copies total, but a number of self-publishers can count on five thousand copies (or more) each year.

Realize, too, that a self-published book often has a better chance of success because it is under the control of one who cares—the author. Dan Poynter, author of *The Self-Publishing Manual* and a self-publisher, has done very well indeed. He sold 130,000 copies of a book called *Hang Gliding* that reportedly took him two months of writing time. One can only wonder what sales of the book would have been if it had been published by a large company!

There is the case of a successful lawyer in the Midwest who finished a novel and sent it off to a likely major publisher. After six months of waiting, her manuscript was finally returned. Undaunted, she sent it to another publisher. An incredible year-and-a-half passed, and then she finally received another rejection.

What did she do? Simple. She published her book herself, doing the artwork and handling its printing and distribution. Her book started selling and soon attracted a West Coast agent who signed the self-published author-lawyer as a client. Her agent sold the paperback rights for a large sum of money.

Vladimir Lange, M.D., self-published his book *Be A Survivor: Your Guide to Breast Cancer Treatment.* He set up a book signing at a popular bookstore and hawked the new title at a medical trade show. Less than one month after the book's initial release, sales were booming. The book went back to the presses for another five-thousand-unit run.

The point is, despite the risk, self-publishing can be a way to success with the major publishers and quite possibly a very profitable way.

How Much Money Do Self-Publishers Make?

While it's impossible to provide accurate forecasts for self-publishing profit scenarios, certain general assumptions can be made. The following table was taken from a self-publisher's business plan, based on current cost of goods and quantified distribution forecasts:

Self-Publishing Payback Scenarios

RPPU	Units	Editing	Writing	Printing	Marketing	Distr. Costs	Total Costs	Gross Rev	Net Profit
$19.95	5,000	$1,500	$7,000	$11,250	$20,000	$29,925	$ 69,675	$ 99,750	$ 30,075
$19.95	10,000	$1,500	$7,000	$17,300	$35,000	$59,850	$120,650	$199,500	$ 78,850
$29.95	5,000	$1,500	$7,000	$11,250	$25,000	$44,925	$ 89,675	$149,750	$ 60,075
$29.95	10,000	$1,500	$7,000	$17,300	$40,000	$89,850	$155,650	$299,500	$143,850

Note: Writing fee is estimated based on the time an author invests in a self-publishing project. A self-publisher sells direct, through an independent distributor at 30 percent distribution cost, and deep discount sales at 50–60 percent off retail. RPPU stands for retail price per unit.

Is There a Future Bundling Books and CD-ROMs Together?

For several years, publishers have experimented with adding value to their book titles by attaching CD-ROMs to the inside back covers of books. The books were then sold to the standard wholesale, retail, and online markets, in the hopes that the combined bundle would jump-start sales, or in the least, give their books a sales advantage over competing products. Unfortunately, publishers (large and small) have been disappointed by the results. The extra revenue the publisher gained from either a higher book price or an increase in book sales was offset by the increased cost of producing the book/CD-ROM bundle. In fact, many publishers pushing book/CD-ROM bundles made *less* profit than they made previously!

Noted media consultant Ben Tenn observes: "The idea of combining books with CD-ROM seems logical but not necessarily viable. If a book sells for a price, and the CD-ROM sells for a price, the combined 'bundle' must therefore sell for a high price, which is likely to reduce sales. In addition, the book and the CD should each stand on their own as product, meaning you are selling the same content twice, only on different media.

"Few bookstores, if any, have welcomed CD-ROM. And if they offer any (for sale), it is low-end budget, not high-priced, frontline product, even if it is in categories you would expect them to carry like reference. Bookstores have not embraced nonprint categories, even VHS, and the early tests of trying CD-ROM, as Borders did a couple of years ago, have been canceled or dramatically reduced."

Waterside's Margot Maley, whose agency sets up mostly computer book deals, echoes some of what Tenn says: "The retail channels are familiar with the book/CD bundle because of the many computer books that now come with CD-ROMs. However, they are being much more selective, even in computer publishing, because the books that include CD-ROMs are at least $10 more expensive and many of the CD-ROMs that have been added to computer books have been total schlock that adds no value for the reader.

"It's a bit trickier to convince general nonfiction publishers to put a CD-ROM in the back of their books. They've been burned by many that didn't sell as well as they thought they would. It does help to have a finished product to demo. It also depends on the type of book. Is it a medical reference? A sports book? CD-ROMs that are not associated with computer books have typically done better as stand-alone products sold through multimedia distributors and not through book distributors."

Strong Distribution Is Essential to Your Success

Distribution still has a long way to go in American book publishing. A grim reality all authors should understand is the fact that the budget is larger for the lead books on a publisher's list, the promotion plan for these main books is more elaborate, and the planning is more precise.

The advance order of a bookstore may well be the only order a book is going to get. Some books are lucky to be distributed to airports, but these are usually bestselling titles only. One retail outlet for books is the supermarket. A number of books are sold there, but again they are the lead titles and usually mass-market paperbacks. The archaic system of distribution may hopefully improve in the early years of the twenty-first century, and there are signs that this is happening already.

To grow in the industry, publishers must find additional outlets where books can be sold. One publishing executive advises: "The more books you sell, the more books you publish. So, unless you want to stay at a certain level, you must find secondary channels to sell your product." For some publishers that has meant distribution to gift shops, specialty stores, gourmet shops, fabric stores, and also more book-club sales.

As one distribution authority puts it: "Good promotion and publicity for a book may be wasted if the distribution has been poor. The effectiveness of promotion, publicity, and advertising can help sales greatly but depends on how well the book has been placed in the stores."

The new electronic market for books is a healthy plus for the distribution phase of publishing. One publisher, Amacom, for example, is launching a series on *The Get-Ahead Toolkit*, which is a book and CD-ROM combination meant to teach basic skills to business managers.

Amacom's Irene Majuk recounts: "We were aware of problems other publishers experienced in selling CD-ROMs in bookstores, so early on we conducted market research with booksellers and software stores. We learned that to be successful in bookstores, the package would need to fit on the shelf with other books and be browsable the way a book is." The key word is "browsable."

Some very sharp minds in publishing have been working diligently to improve the entire distribution system, and everyone in the business can only hope for the best as the early twenty-first century unfolds. Distribution is bound to get better, if only slowly.

Electronic Books: The New Format for the Twenty-First Century

Today's computer-savvy authors have one distinct advantage over their typewriter-bound colleagues: they can earn additional revenue by exercising the electronic rights clauses in their contracts. In fact, one of the authors of this book has made more money from licensing the electronic rights to his material than he has made from his standard book advances and royalties combined!

How can you make money from exercising the electronic rights clause in your book publishing contract? It's easier than you think. Before we discuss the terms and techniques you should use to increase your book revenue, let's take a look at what kind of electronic format we are talking about.

What Is an Electronic Book?

Back in 1993, photojournalist Rick Smolan and adventurer Robyn Davidson set out to create an electronic companion to a coffee-table book they were planning to produce about Davidson's seven-and-a-half-month journey on camelback across the Australian desert. The resulting electronic book, *From Alice to Ocean*, was hailed by critics at the time as one of the finest examples of how multimedia technology could be combined with the written word to create a bold new user experience.

Interactive Bureau, a New York digital studio, spent three years converting 26,989 pages of each issue of the *Craftsman* magazine into an electronic and enhanced replica on CD-ROM that includes a searchable index featuring 3,639 abstracts that are linked to corresponding articles. The *Craftsman* was the bible of the arts and crafts movement in the United States between 1900 and 1920. The newly released electronic book provides a rare glimpse into our country's past and serves as an historic preservation of the antiquarian society.

Electronic books add a new dimension to the printed word. The content of the book doesn't change so much as its *presentation*, along with what the reader can *do* with the material. Electronic books not only combine standard book elements such as text, photographs, charts, graphs, and illustrations, but add video, sound, interactive worksheets, and animation. These new texts are delivered on floppy disk, on CD-ROM, or via Adobe Acrobat PDF (portable document format) files over the Internet and are viewed on the reader/viewer's computer screen.

On the surface, this enriched content is what makes electronic books different from their paperbound counterparts. However, upon closer examination, electronic books engage the reader in a bold new way. Readers of electronic texts can interact with the material, which requires that authors have a deep understanding about the concept of interactivity and how interactive multimedia experiences engage more than one sense to stimulate the reader. This idea isn't new. Comenius was an early pedagogue who, in the 1600s, applied theory to practice by developing a textbook for children that used both pictorial and verbal presentations as a teaching method.

What is new—what the computer adds to the equation—is the power of participation; the ability to have a reader interact with the material being presented onscreen. Computers have huge advantages in this regard, being able to supply vast quantities of information within a stimulating aural, graphic, and spatial environment while allowing the user to determine the pace or "path" of instruction. The linearity of a printed book is no longer a constraint as electronic texts allow the user to choose how they would like to navigate the material. That is, the user can flip the "pages" of the electronic book in linear order (just like reading a standard book) or "jump forward" to the material that is most relevant to their needs.

It is the author's task to help the publisher's content planning team enhance the text by adding the right interactive components to the mix in order to produce the best electronic book possible.

Producing an Electronic Book

The easiest, most cost-efficient method for producing an electronic book is to create a PDF version of a book that has already been designed and laid out in Quark XPress or PageMaker. Adobe PDF allows the content creator to capture the exact look and feel of the printed page. It's a simple conversion procedure. With the click of a mouse, a book can be transformed into a PDF document. Layers of interactivity are then added to the electronic manuscript. The resulting PDF file can be distributed on floppy disk, CD-ROM, or downloaded directly from the Web.

For example, Jon Samsel's electronic PDF book *The Killer Content Workbook* needed to teach its readers how to mine their creative ideas and turn those ideas into something they could use in their businesses. The book version discusses how we are all creative, suggesting ways in which readers can mine their ideas, and how they can put their ideas down on paper.

The interactive PDF version of the book addresses these same issues but adds some new features. The user can click on an onscreen image to call up a worksheet that demonstrates the author's concepts. It then prompts the reader to "fill in the blanks," compelling the reader to do something with his or her newfound knowledge.

Another feature of *The Killer Content Workbook* is its use of multimedia. In the right-hand column of each page of the original book, a reader can read an inspirational quote by a famous artist. The electronic version added a new dimension—the reader can not only read the quote, he or she can hear the quote read aloud by clicking on the phrase.

The enhanced features of an electronic book such as *The Killer Content Workbook* can actually enrich the learning experience for the reader. Perhaps that's why Apple Computer licensed the electronic book so that its 15,000 worldwide developers could read—and interact with—the material.

Another electronic book publishing mechanism is the Versabook system, a technology solution for publishing multimedia digital reference works. The system enables consumers to download digital reference books over the Internet onto their personal computers in a matter of minutes. The system has attracted the attention of publishing behemoths such as Random House, Simon & Schuster, Merriam-Webster, NTC Publishing, PRIMEDIA Reference and World Almanac, and Oxford University Press, who are now using the system.

Secure Your Electronic Rights!

Most authors can increase the amount of money they earn from writing books if they simply negotiate better contracts. By "better," we're specifically zeroing in on the electronic rights clause in your publishing contract. Traditionally, book publishers control this clause, yet seldom exercise the right to use it. They want to control it because of a fear that some new technology may come along that will allow publishers to make money by publishing these newfangled electronic manuscripts. Well guess what? Not only does that new technology already exist, but most publishers don't know how to make money using it!

Interactive PDF books and electronic books on CD-ROM have been around for several years now. The problem is, the book publishers don't know how to build a sustainable revenue stream by publishing such electronic tomes. There is not a mass-market demand for these type of books as yet. Consequently, most publishers control these electronic rights even though they have no short-term plans to produce any electronic derivatives.

Let's take a look at the language found in many standard book publishing agreements. This is what is known as a "We own your soul" clause, because it encompasses all forms of media, known and unknown, and forever:

CLAUSE #1
Author, on behalf of himself and his heirs, executors, administrators, successors, and assigns, exclusively grants, assigns, and
otherwise transfers to Publisher and its licensees, successors,
and assigns, all right, title, and interest in and to the Work,
throughout the world, in perpetuity, and in all media and
forms of expressions now known or hereafter devised, including but not limited to all copyrights therein (and any and all
extensions and renewals thereof) for the full term of such
copyrights, and all secondary and subsidiary rights therein.

If an author insists on retaining his or her electronic rights, many
small- to medium-sized publishers may specify that they are making a
book deal only and will insert a clause similar to this one into their
book publishing agreements:

CLAUSE #2
All rights not specifically granted to the Publisher are reserved
to the Author, including but not limited to electronic rights, which
are defined as rights in the digitized form of works that can be
encoded, stored, and retrieved from such media as computer
disks, CD-ROMs, computer databases, and network servers.

While the above clause grants full electronic rights to the author,
the publisher has no vested interest in promoting any form of the
book that is not printed and bound in the traditional format.

Another option for writers is to allow the publisher to control the
electronic rights as long as the author shares handsomely in the future
royalties or licensing fees generated from the sale or lease of these
rights. This way, if the publisher does want to exploit the rights, both
the publisher and author can share in the profits.

Let's take a look at an electronic rights clause from an actual book
contract where the author and publisher share in the electronic rights
revenue:

CLAUSE #3
Grant of Electronic Rights. Author agrees to grant Publisher
the exclusive right to transfer Electronic Site License "leases"

and other "leases" outside of the conventional channels of distribution in the book industry. "Electronic Site License," as used in this Agreement, refers to the Publisher's creating and "leasing" an electronic version of the Work to post on a Third-Party's proprietary online site or a proprietary Intranet server, for a specific period of time for a predetermined fee.

Publisher shall report promptly to the Author any licenses entered into whenever their share of royalty is to be one hundred dollars ($100) or more. Fifty percent (50%) of the net proceeds ("net" being defined as after the subtraction of any expenses, such as for agents or designers to develop the electronic version) shall be paid to the Author (regardless of whether the advance has an unpaid balance) up to the Author's receipt of $7,500 from such Electronic Site Licenses, after which thirty percent (30%) of the net proceeds shall be paid to the Author.

What's great about this electronic rights clause is that it spreads the wealth to both author and publisher while giving the publisher an incentive to sell. If the publisher is able to license the material to an interested third party, everybody wins.

Authors who buy Adobe Acrobat and learn how to use it can even produce the work for the publisher. Many publishers are not very computer literate and authors with this skill can make a few thousand dollars building electronic versions of their books for their publishers to sell.

Licensing fees vary from company to company and deal to deal. If a computer company wants to license an electronic book on Web design to run on its corporate Intranet, a system where 10,000 employees will have access to the material, a licensing fee of $10,000 would not be unusual.

How much of the $10,000 licensing fee would the author receive? Using Clause #3 above as our guide, we would first need to subtract the cost of producing the electronic PDF version of the book—say $2,000 from the licensing fee. That leaves $8,000 to be split two ways—$4,000 for the publisher and $4,000 for the author. Not a bad payday considering most author advances are in the $3,000–$10,000 range. And that $4,000 licensing fee is from one buyer. Imagine the money an author can make if the publisher licenses the electronic book to two or three other buyers!

If you are an author who still owns all electronic rights to a book, your tenacity and hard work can really pay off. Produce an electronic book yourself and reap all the rewards! Launch a Web site and sell your electronic book online. Get an agent to license your electronic book. Copy your book to floppy disk and sell it via direct mail. Syndicate your electronic book to online newspapers, book clubs, or other commercial sites that need fresh content. The sky's the limit!

‒‒‒✦‒‒‒

CHAPTER 14

From Author to Marketer: What to Do When Your Manuscript Is Done

The incredible thing about the great author Margaret Mitchell is that she never thought or even considered the possibility of publication for the novel she worked on for years. During the late 1920s, she had to stay in bed several years for health reasons. To amuse herself, she wrote about Atlanta, the Civil War, and lost herself creating characters like Scarlett O'Hara and Rhett Butler.

Mitchell worked on her manuscript for one reason—her own interest and amusement. It was years later, after a Macmillan editor heard about her work and came to Atlanta, that *Gone with the Wind* was published (in 1936).

Strategies for Approaching the Marketplace

Margaret Mitchell is a strong example of an author who never thought about the marketplace while writing her novel about the old South. She didn't think it was any good. What a far cry that is compared with today's aggressive authors who pull out all the stops in marketing their books. Some authors of today even plan strategic campaigns to place their manuscripts.

The first thing an author should be aware of is that it's a buyer's market. Everyone and his brother's cousin is writing, and that means most of the better publishers have a much wider choice. Publishers today no doubt reach for the rejection forms or "thank you, but it's not right for our list" reply much quicker. After all, they have stacks and stacks of other manuscripts and proposals sitting on most editorial desks. This buyer's market atmosphere will continue through the early years of the twenty-first century and may well become entrenched.

As discussed earlier, one of the best strategies for approaching the marketplace is simply to let a worthy and capable agent do it for you. This allows the author to focus on writing and not have to think about marketing. Effective agents know which publishers are the right ones for a given book, so you don't waste valuable time sending work to the wrong companies. And the agent can get you a decision a great deal sooner, whereas if you try one publisher at a time, on your own, it could take years to get even a handful of decisions.

But for most new authors, getting a quality agent is about twenty times harder than finding a publisher. This puts new authors back at square one and often results in the authors giving up or marketing their work themselves as best they can.

A strange but very true fact about today's publishing industry is that authors with up to fifty published books, including several or more bestsellers, cannot get an agent to represent them. It's a paradox and proves that the so-called importance of a track record of published works does not really count for much anymore. Many of the top publishers and editors simply won't consider anything unless it comes in from a powerhouse agent with clout. Powerful agents have, to a large extent, taken over the industry. They have become the gatekeepers today instead of editors.

Other leading editors focus their time on big-name authors and proven commodities. It's a catch-22 that frustrates a lot of authors, driving many of them out of publishing. Every now and then, however, a newcomer manages to slip in with good timing, a great proposal or manuscript, and lots of luck.

Another strategy is to already know someone in publishing or have a friend or relative who does. Networking may get your foot in the door. Some patient authors have even obtained positions in publishing, in publicity, advertising, marketing, rights, or general office work, and then proceeded to show their work to contacts already made.

It's helpful to read the trade journals and to attend publishing conferences and conventions. All of this helps to keep you well informed on what is going on in the industry, what the current trends are, types of books being bought and published, and contact names at various publishing houses.

A number of writers believe attending conferences for authors is a waste of time. Others claim they have made some contacts this way and actually later sold one or more books to editors and agents who attend the better author conferences.

Remember, too, that you can always pick up the telephone and call an editor, whether it irritates them or not. You can send a snail-paced letter that takes a week or ten days to get there. You can fax them, send a telegram, or try some unusual stunt to get their attention. A combination of these methods applied persistently should bring you some success or, at the very least, more knowledge about the way the business works. Authors in the New York area have been known to eat at the same restaurants editors frequent in hopes of meeting one or more.

If and when one of your books goes over the top and hits the blockbuster level, assuming there is enough publicity, editors and agents may come after you. Nothing gets their attention, makes them sit up and take notice, like a new author who just turned out a blockbuster. They will then find you.

Innovative Ways to Promote Your Book

There are two types of promotion: what your publisher can do for the book and what you can accomplish yourself. Anything you can do for each of your books will help.

The following promotions have worked for many authors:

- Do all in your power to get on local radio and television programs. You can write the station, one or more specific talk-show personalities, or even go to the station in person. Ask for an appointment with the radio personality, program director, or public relations director, for example.

  Nothing pushes book sales up like radio/television author interviews, and the better known or more popular the program is, the more sales it can mean. Most publishers will not line up such interviews for you unless you're a meganame or well-known author. That means it's up to you. Listen or watch these programs and try to come up with a reason tied in with your book why they should interview you.

  If there is any way you could get yourself on *Today, Good Morning America,* or *Oprah Winfrey,* go for it. Your book sales could go soaring through the stratosphere.

- Many large city newspapers have book columns or entertainment section news that could feature your book. Go by the newspapers and try to meet the columnists or department editors who interview authors.

  Look for some angle that a magazine or newspaper editor could use to publicize your book. Will your book help the reader in some way, perhaps to get a better job, save time, become healthier, more fit, or learn a business concept?

- If you know how to write an article, consider the idea of writing a feature about your own book. It is possible that a national, regional, or local magazine or newspaper might use it. If your book is on a timely subject, chances are even greater that your article will be used.

- Contact any and all trade journals and publications about your book. Many fields have their own trade magazines, so check it out.

- Tell everyone about your book and write letters about it to anyone you feel could help promote and publicize it.

- Suggest to the larger bookstores, both the chains and independents, that you could do autograph sessions and sign copies of your new book. Offer to speak at bookstores because they sometimes have author guests do this and answer questions about their book topic.

- Many authors don't keep after their publishers to promote their books. Whether it results in anything or not, it's worth encouraging your publisher to get behind your book more. Offer to tour for your book or suggest at least a mini-tour.

  A number of sharp authors have traveled across America visiting bookstores, radio and television stations, and newspapers to promote their books. In many cases, it made the difference between just another book and a bestseller.

  There are simply too many books being published each year (60,000 and counting) to do nothing for your book once it is published. If you, the author, don't promote it, nobody else will (and, unfortunately, this can also include your publisher).

- Tap the huge marketing opportunity via the Internet. According to Penguin chief executive Michael Lynton, "The Internet could make backlist titles much more widely available to buyers. It might be well worth it to have your own Web site for promoting your book or books. Sales of Penguin books through Amazon.com were over $10 million for last year."

  According to the Department of Commerce's three-hundred-page paper "The Emerging Digital Economy," Internet traffic is doubling every one hundred days. Between 1993 and 1997, the number of Internet users rocketed from 3 million to more than 100 million.

  Authors who are Internet-savvy will have a competitive advantage over their computer-weary counterparts. If you are not already on the Net, if you don't use e-mail or have your own Web page, it's not too late to get onboard the Internet express train.

- Write a direct sales letter in which you tell about yourself and your book. Send the letter to a list of radio and television program directors, producers, and talk-show personalities who may be receptive to having you as a guest author. Send your sales letter to a wide variety of stations. In fact, send your sales letter to anyone you think might help promote your book.

- Consider "self-syndicating" a feature article or review about your book. You can get the names of a great many newspaper editors in yearly syndicate directories published by *Editor and Publisher*.

- Work up an oral presentation in which you talk about your book; for example, discuss why you wrote it. Prepare a professional-looking pamphlet highlighting the features of your talk and telling something about your background. Have a number of copies printed and then send them to anyone and everyone who might book you on a program as a speaker. A number of authors do very nicely working as speakers in between their writing projects or even while they are writing.

- Arrange a book release party for your new book. Invite friends, business associates, key book industry professionals, and perhaps even the general public. This is a fun way to announce the release of your new book and it starts the word-of-mouth process.

- Contact your local libraries and let them know that an author in the area just had a book published. Many libraries will invite authors to speak on your subject of expertise or host a reading of a book chapter. Again, this is another way to spread the word about your new book.

- Frequent online chat rooms and newsgroups and offer your expert advice. The online world is a great environment for spreading awareness for your book and/or professional services. Be careful not to blatantly pitch your wares, as the online world has strict rules of etiquette—no unsolicited advertising or promotions are allowed. Authors who ignore the Internet's professional protocol risk being "spammed" by concerned cybercitizens (spamming means getting bombarded with angry e-mail).

  Authors who visit chat rooms or newsgroups and contribute *meaningful* information and advice (and casually mention that the reason they are authorities on a subject is because they have written a book on the subject) are likely to increase awareness of their books.

• Contact the wire services about your new book. Send them a traditional press release via mail or e-mail them a text version of your release. Most major newspapers and e-zines (online magazines) subscribe to one or more of the news wire services. If your story is picked up by one of these news wires, it can instantly be picked up by hundreds, if not thousands, of wire service subscribers. The major wire services are:

Associated Press (AP)
50 Rockefeller Plaza
New York, NY 10020
Tel. (212) 621-1500
Web site: *www.ap.org*

United Press International (UPI)
1510 H Street NW #600
Washington, D.C. 20005
Tel. (202) 898-8000
Web site: *www.upi.com*

Reuters Information Services
1700 Broadway
New York, NY 10019
Tel. (212) 603-3300
Web site: *www.reuters.com*

Publicity Stunts

Sometimes clever and unusual publicity stunts can send sales of a book soaring. If you are an imaginative and somewhat daring author, you might consider dreaming up some kind of publicity stunt to attract attention to your book. With 60,000 or more new books coming out each year, the more attention you can get for your book, the better chance it will have to break out.

A man who ran for governor of Tennessee walked across the entire state. He received regular and continuous publicity for the walk and was shown talking to people all along the way. Stories about him were featured on many evening news programs. He made a mark on his map at the end of each day to show where he had stopped, then resumed his walk at his marker the next morning. It was an effective idea and worked well for him.

Some publicity stunts of course take a bit more daring and nerve than others. If your book title or subject lends itself to it, consider wearing some kind of costume when you visit bookstores. Focus on stunts that will bring your book attention and favorable publicity.

If you like the idea of wearing some kind of costume that calls attention to your book, think about combining that with a walk across your state, region, tristate area, or the entire country. This of course also goes for authors overseas.

Some authors plan elaborate and detailed publicity stunts. When writing your book, if possible, keep alert. There may be clues in your book for a possible publicity stunt you could do. The questions to ask include the following:

- Are there any unusual ways to advertise and promote my book?

- What could I do to attract favorable attention and publicity for my book?

- Could I arrange to get any local, regional, or national celebrity to plug my book?

- Is there anything unique, timely, shocking, or newsworthy about the book that might get me an interview/guest appearance on major radio/television programs or any of the lesser known, regional, or local programs?

Some ten years ago, a friendly customer visited a bookstore in Oxford, Mississippi. He told the owner of the store that he was writing a book. The owner thought he was just another wannabe writer, but later the man returned to report that his book was being published. He told the owner he needed to sell five hundred copies.

The author asked if he could do an autograph session in the store. All the young man's friends, relatives, and neighbors were invited to the signing. The result was fifty-three copies sold. The young author was John Grisham, and the book he signed that day was *A Time to Kill*.

The bottom line is to think of anything and everything you can do with regard to promotion and publicity stunts that will help your book make a strong performance in the marketplace. Who knows? Sometimes even a wacky publicity stunt might skyrocket the sales of your book and get your career as an author moving.

Get in Touch with Newspaper Columnists

There are columns written on all kinds of subjects. Your book may be of interest to the readers of columns on lifestyles, business, money matters, self-help subjects, cooking, real estate, marriage, religion, or whatever.

The circulation of many columns runs in the hundreds of thousands and even the millions in some cases. A mention of your book by the columnist could be a real promotional shot in the arm for it. According to reports, a positive mention or endorsement of a book in certain columns has brought a windfall in sales.

Above all, don't depend on your publisher to contact columnists. If it's going to happen, the author has to make it happen. L. P. Wilbur had the enthusiastic endorsement for an earlier book from no less than Clive Cussler, a mega-blockbuster author in the multimillion class. The publisher was told about the endorsement and given the information necessary to contact Cussler. The publisher was given the written quote and endorsement to use. So what happened? The publisher ignored the endorsement and published the book without it. So the truth is that today's author must do much more than just write the book; you must also promote it and do everything possible to give it a chance. If you don't, then the odds that it may die on the vine increase considerably. You cannot count on the publisher to promote it. Some publishers do token promotion while others do next to nothing. The only sure way to get big-time promotion and backing for a book from most publishers is to become a blockbuster, megabucks author. Then they will pull out all the stops.

CHAPTER 1 5

———◆———

How to Use the Internet as a Sales and Marketing Tool

Authors, repeat after me: *The Internet is my friend. The Internet can help me publicize my book to millions of readers. The Internet is the world's largest sales and marketing tool.*

The word is out that the Internet can help authors market and sell their books. Why is it then that so few authors utilize the Internet to help them "guerrilla market" their book titles? Why are so many authors hesitant to use the electronic medium to hawk their wares?

The answer is simple. From the Internet to radio talk shows, from *Oprah* to *Larry King Live*: book authors are just plain lousy at marketing. And nothing they do—short of buying all their own books—is going to increase the number of books they sell. What is an author to do, you ask? Open your eyes! Learn how to self-promote and market your book using the Internet as a high-tech sales tool.

Internet consultant Charles Austin sums up the importance of the Internet with this advice: "Embrace the Web. It's like an express train—you can either jump on board or it will run you down."

167

Help Your Publisher Market Your Book

Let's face it, today's publishers are having a hard time devoting proper sales and marketing attention to any one book. Most publishers promote a catalog of titles each sales cycle, and authors are lucky if their publishers arrange a few book signings or radio interviews for them. It's not that the publishers don't want to promote your book. Of course they do. They want to make money—to see a return on their investment—just as much as you do. But the publisher looks at book publishing as a *business*. They approach the release of a book as a *function of their business* and the sale of a book as a *business transaction*.

But for you, the author, your entire career and financial livelihood may be on the line when a new book rolls off the press. Marketing a book is not a simple business proposition. It's a matter of survival.

If authors were Boy Scouts, they'd be lost in the wilderness. Marketing is not a natural instinct; it's learned behavior. Most authors are great at putting words to paper, jawing about grammar over a cup of coffee, attending inspirational seminars, and discussing the finer points of literary theory. But those same wordsmiths rarely invest that same time and energy learning how to promote their writing careers. They're too busy doing other things. Authors need to learn some new skills to compete in today's rough-and-tumble book market.

Bestselling author James Halperin uses the Internet and e-mail for promotional purposes: "I enjoy interacting with readers. My publisher [Ballantine Books] created Web sites for both *The Truth Machine* (*www.truthmachine.com*) and *The First Immortal* (*www.firstimmortal.com*), and I regularly contribute to discussions on those sites, although not actively enough to suit my publisher, of course!"

Halperin also encourages his readers to interact with him via electronic mail. The exchange of e-mail helps build relationships with his readers—and, hopefully, will lead many readers to become regular buyers of his books. Halperin recently concocted an interesting challenge to his readers: "I encourage reader feedback. In the introduction to my book *The First Immortal*, I offer a bounty for any reader who can find a factual error in the manuscript. I offer a scarce Ivy Press first edition of *The Truth Machine* to each reader who is the first to point out a scientific or factual error which I subsequently correct. My e-mail address is listed in the book, along with the mailing address for Ballantine Books."

There are several ways an author can use the Internet to help promote a book. Ideas include creating a digital press kit, promoting your title to online bookstores, providing third-party endorsements, launching your own Web site, positioning yourself as a leading authority in your field, launching a digital propaganda campaign, and getting listed on all the online search engines.

Let's take a closer look at each of these ideas.

Create a Digital Press Kit

Authors need to prepare several essential elements as part of a press kit so that the publisher has no excuse for not developing an electronic marketing campaign around their books. These elements include an author photo (in GIF and JPEG formats), an author biography (one or two paragraphs), a book cover (in GIF or JPEG), a book excerpt (several pages to an entire chapter), the book's technical specs (price, ISBN number, and publisher name and phone number), ten possible interview questions that a radio host or journalist might pose, and author contact information.

Promote Your Title to Online Bookstores

A great way to promote your book is to announce the title on all the online bookstores. You'll need to provide electronic versions of the book cover, technical book specs, and a book synopsis. Once your book is logged into the online bookstore's database, millions of book lovers will be able to find and order your title. The eight major online bookstores are listed below.

- Amazon.com: Billed as the "earth's biggest bookstore," customers can search the company's online catalog by author, title, subject, or keyword. Sold at discounts of up to 40 percent, books are ordered directly from distributors or publishers after the customer selects a particular book; most are delivered within two to three days. Amazon.com also offers free book recommendations, e-mail notification services of new books, and author interviews. This is a great destination!

- barnesandnoble.com: Barnes and Noble is the top bookseller in the United States, operating more than 1,000 stores, including over 400 superstores (Barnes and Noble Booksellers, Bookstop, and Bookstar) and almost 580 mall stores (B. Dalton Bookseller, Doubleday Book Shops, and Scribner's Bookstores). In addition, the company runs a leading direct-mail bookselling business and has its own book publishing business. This is another great online destination!

- Booksnow.com: Books Now, a division of DataMark Holding, provides the book-buying public the opportunity to shop from home, through its Virtual Bookstore and through its strategic alliances with hundreds of national magazines such as *Field and Stream, Cosmopolitan,* and *Town and Country.* This is a fairly good destination for inline book customers.

- Booksamillion.com: Books-A-Million is one of the dominant book retailers in the Southeast and the fourth largest book chain in the United States. The company operates more than 165 bookstores in seventeen states, including about 110 superstores (operated under the Books-A-Million name). Most of its traditional stores are located in regional malls and operate under the Bookland name. Books-A-Million is a wholesaler of bargain books to bookstore chains and of a range of books to independent bookstores and mass merchandisers. Another good destination for online book customers.

- Books.com: Books.com is the original online bookstore founded in 1991. Originally known as Book Stacks, Books.com is a virtual bookstore that carries about millions of titles, most of which are discounted 20–40 percent. When you visit Books.com, you can browse the "shelves" and search for books by author, title, subject, keyword, or ISBN. Choose your titles, place your order and your books will be shipped directly to your home or office. As a special bonus, when you purchase books from Books.com, you earn credits, called Bookmarks, which can be redeemed for free books. The Books.com Web site is functional but due for a makeover.

- Borders.com: Borders is the second largest bookstore operator in the United States (after Barnes and Noble) with stores in all fifty states. It operates over 1,100 retail stores: Waldenbooks (mall-based bookstore chain), Borders (books and music superstores), Planet Music (CD superstores), and Books etc. (United Kingdom–based bookstores). Borders.com launched a full-service online bookstore in 1998—comparable to rivals Amazon.com and barnesandnoble.com.

- Crownbooks.com: Crown Books operates about 170 bookstores across the United States, primarily in big cities such as Los Angeles, Chicago, and Washington, D.C. The company's Classic Crown Books stores offer fiction, nonfiction, bestsellers, cookbooks, children's books, magazines, and books on tape; its Super Crown Books locations offer greeting cards, gifts, and games, in addition to a wide range of books. Crownbooks.com is not in the same league as its competitors; it needs a renovation.

- Clbooks.com: Computer Literacy is the online version of the popular technical book chain. It stocks over 20,000 technical books—from the hottest bestsellers to the most difficult-to-locate technical references. If you like technology books, you'll like this site.

Many online bookstores allow readers to comment about the books they've read and then post their comments alongside the standard book data. Consumers who are browsing a book title may choose to read what other buyers thought of the book before they purchase it. Consumers like this feature because they feel these reader comments allow them to make a more informed buying decision.

We asked author James Halperin for his thoughts on the reader comments found at Amazon.com about his book *The Truth Machine*. The reader comments range from deep praise to extreme distaste. Halperin reflects:

In retrospect, through the sieve of time, I have come to the conclusion that they are both right. A lot of it has to do with whether readers like the central idea or hate it. The political and scientific ideas I explore in this book will cause a reaction—one way or another, which I think is a plus for the book. Even if you hate my ideas, at least the book made you think.

The truth is, my opinions—especially political opinions—are constantly evolving.

Some things I wrote about in *The Truth Machine* have been misinterpreted. For example, people think that I'm pro–Swift and Sure death penalty. Give me a break! Swift and Sure is a pragmatic solution to a problem (in our society) that defies pragmatic solutions. The concept was presented as a choice among evils.

As far as the writing style, the dialogue is quite wooden because, frankly, I didn't know how to write back then! It was my first work of fiction and the characters were somewhat one-dimensional. However, I note with some pride that in spite of this, I somehow managed to create a simple, compelling story that strikes a chord with a lot of people. A very cinematic story.

So far, I've read every piece of e-mail that has ever been sent to me and responded to every person who has read one of my books. I get e-mail from people who have read *The Truth Machine* thirty times. I get e-mail from parents who tell me that their kids were slackers who weren't interested in anything—until they read *The Truth Machine* and started studying because they wanted to be like Pete Armstrong (the book's lead character) and change the world. I'm still shocked to get feedback like that, and it makes me feel great.

Provide Third-Party Endorsements

There's nothing like the implied endorsement of a nonbiased third party to dispel customer skepticism about a book. Here's how you "build" an endorsement:

Think of the top five most influential people you know, send them your completed manuscript (before it comes off the press), get their feedback, and mold the most positive comments into a favorable endorsement that sells.

For example, a nonfiction book about government cover-ups, UFO conspiracies, and alien autopsies might read as follows:

"This book is a chilling reminder to all Americans that what we see and read in the media should not always be taken at face value. The authors walk the reader through previously unseen evidence, painstakingly piecing together a global space odyssey that will shock and amaze you. I highly recommend this book."

—Randolph McAllister, *Director of the Area 54 Science Institute*

Launch Your Own Web Site

Many authors mistakenly assume that Web sites are *only* destinations created for businesses looking to market their goods and services. That's not true! Thousands (if not millions) of individuals maintain their own Web sites on the Internet. What do they use them for? For some, it's a vanity item. These people don't have much to say other than, "Look! I have my own Web page." However, many people (especially authors) have a lot to say, and the Web is the perfect publishing vehicle for them. You might say that the Web is a self-publisher's dream medium.

Why should an author have a personal Web site? How about using the site to promote your book title? How about using your site to build a community meeting center for like-minded folk with similar interests? Or, if you're having trouble getting a publisher to pick up your book title, why not let people read excerpts of your book and give you feedback? This feedback can be used to get publishers interested in your title. That's what James Halperin did with his first book, *The Truth Machine*, which went on to be published by a major publishing house.

"With seemingly few options available, I decided to publish the book (*The Truth Machine*) myself," claims Halperin. "I lined up a printer and a distributor, and I even posted the book on the Web. The deal with the Web was that anybody could read the book as long as they completed a series of six surveys (inserted between chapters). I never really advertised my Web site. I think I sent out one bulk e-mailing and posted notices on quite a few newsgroups. My Web site was hit 15,000 times in three and one-half months. I collected 10,000 reader surveys. It was amazing."

Position Yourself as a Leading Authority in Your Field

When you write a book and that book is published, like it or not you become known as an expert in the topic of your book. As an authority in your subject area, many new and exciting marketing opportunities await you. For example, book authors can:

- Teach an online class (using their book as a textbook).

- Write an introduction to another author's book (exposing you and your book credits to a new audience).

- Contribute to online discussions and cyberseminars (picking up some extra cash from event organizers while exposing your book to potential buyers).

- Guest-host online chat sessions sponsored by one of the many "channels" offered on commercial online services such as America Online and CompuServe (again, more exposure for your book).

- Write an online article relating to your area of expertise and sell it to online newspapers, magazines, organizations, or other commercial Web sites that may have a need for your informative viewpoint (you get paid *and* get free exposure for your book).

Launch a Digital Propaganda Campaign

The more consumers know about your book, the more it will sell. And online publicity (or propaganda campaign, depending on how you look at it) is an essential component for any author looking to spread the word on a new book title. How do authors publicize their books online? There are several techniques an author should know about:

- *Chat Till You're Blue in the Face:* Enter an online chat room and start discussions with like-minded folk looking for information on your book topic. Or visit Usenet newsgroups and Internet mailing lists and announce your book. Don't do the hard sell; just casually mention your book when people are searching for more information on the topic of your book. Sales often develop from authors who know how to reach out to would-be consumers, engage them, and build relationships.

- *Start an Electronic Newsletter:* Collect the e-mail addresses of friends, associates, and potential customers. Send them a brief message (two or three paragraphs) once a month letting them know how your book is selling, where you will be speaking, or what people are saying about your book. Keep in touch with your circle of electronic acquaintances and they will help you market your book through positive word of mouth.

- *Tap into the Power of the Press:* Notify every online newspaper and magazine editor about your book. Set a goal for yourself. Spend at least one evening a week browsing the World Wide Web looking for newspapers, magazines, and information sites that relate to your book's subject matter. Send the editor at each of these online locations a brief press release about your book. Offer to send the editors a digital press kit and a hard copy of the book if they are interested (coordinate this with your publisher). If even ten or twenty of these Web sites decide to mention or review your book, thousands of potential buyers will learn about your book from a reputable third party. A few evenings a month sounds like a small price to pay for more money in your pocket!

Get Listed on All the Online Search Engines

Getting online is easy. Getting people to notice you and your books is not. However, the crafty author can manipulate the system (using Internet search engines) to help increase the odds that a new book, your personal Web site, and/or your publisher's Web site get noticed more often. The more people that know about your books, the more likely they are to purchase them!

For those of you unfamiliar with Internet jargon, a search engine is a service location on the Internet where huge amounts of information are cataloged, such as Web site addresses, reference material, user names, and products information. Most search engines use spider or robot mechanisms that automatically browse the Web twenty-four hours a day. They gather information, link by link, making it easier for Web users to find what they need.

To get the search engines to pay attention to you, submit the URL (uniform resource locator) of your personal Web site or your publisher's Web site to as many search engines as you can. Before you do this, you should make sure to add meta tags to each page of the Web site. Meta tags make it easier for search engines to identify your Web site from the millions of other online destinations. Meta tags are indicators embedded into HTML code used to predetermine what the description and keywords will be for your site. When you use meta tags, you tell search engine spiders to read the description and key-words on your Web site. They catalog that information and make it available to Internet users who perform searches for key words and phrases.

Once you have notified all the search engines where they can find you and your Web site, use the online marketing techniques outlined earlier in this chapter to promote you and your book title.

Some of this online grunt work can be tedious, but the results can be fantastic for your book. So log online and get busy. And good luck!

Where Do You Go from Here?

As the future unfolds, and whatever your connection with books—nonfiction or novels—let your heart and mind and spirit feed on this truth: Nobody in the publishing industry really knows for sure what books will sell and what will capture the public's fancy and attention. In fact, a leading trade journal in the industry recently quoted an editor as saying that some of the major publishers engage in a guessing game as to what will sell rather than depend on editorial judgment.

An author should be true to any inner vision of a book. It's the age-old question: Do you write what is commercial or write the book you want to write? In most cases, authors should write the book in their hearts.

Unless you see yourself as a one-book author, you may well do a number of books in the course of a career and over a period of years. Some books will probably be commercial; others will be experiments and ventures into subject areas or plots that intrigue you. If you continue writing for a number of years, you will sooner or later find your own voice, the genre perhaps that is right for you, your special niche.

The only way to discover these answers is to write. If you are fortunate to work with quality editors, they can help you find some of these answers.

Authors: Custodians of a Proud Heritage

Author Lewis Carroll once said: "Sometimes I've believed as many as six impossible things before breakfast." Poet Robert Frost said, "My life was a risk—and I took it!" Certainly the writer's life requires both imagination and courage.

In the words of David Dortorf, writer, teacher, and book enthusiast, "Nothing is as lonely as the empty page. But the divine spirit moves us to fill it. Homer filled such a page three thousand years ago. We writers are custodians of a proud heritage. We are the bearers of the divine spirit. We must write and write whether it sells or not or is proclaimed unpublished. Authors keep the divine spirit alive. To dare to be creative is to keep the world in something of a state of grace."

Tolstoy was thirty-six when he started *War and Peace*, which took him six years to write. He had a whopping five hundred characters in the novel, and he framed his characters on people he knew or knew of. He used them as models and then added his own imagination.

If and when writing becomes your passion in life, there will be no stopping you, whether it's fiction you write or nonfiction. Even when you are sure you must write, it requires discipline and, on some days, a lot of it. Think of the enormous discipline it took Margaret Mitchell to turn out such a great book, a novel that remains a masterpiece.

You must always keep in mind that editors and publishers can make mistakes. They are human. They may reject an author's book one day and later accept it with or without changes. It's also important not to feel that you must confine your imagination and ability to one subject or one type of book alone. Some authors are meant to do a variety of different books; others become specialists. When an idea grips and compels you to develop it, should you short-circuit it because you have never done that type of book before or done several similar ones?

In other words, authors should be true to themselves and the work they want to do.

Devoting Your Life to a Writing Career

Many newcomers to the writing business know they want to give their lives to their work, but what seems to happen in a great many cases is that they are forced to split their time, especially in the early years, between their love for writing and the need to earn a sure income.

For every early or overnight commercial or literary success, hundreds to thousands of other author hopefuls must weave their way through full- or part-time jobs, perhaps additional education, time spent in trade school or college, possibly being married at the same time and raising a family, and other assorted invasions of time by life. The challenge then becomes to make time for writing in spite of whatever life throws at you. That could mean only getting to write in the evenings, on weekends, getting up several hours earlier to write (before going to a job), staying up well past midnight to knock out more pages on a book in progress, or even working half the night.

If there is one word that sums all this up, it has to be "sacrifice." Deciding to give your life to writing involves much more than the decision; it implies your consent and willingness to sacrifice and endure possible hardship until you are able, if ever, to make a comfortable living from writing.

To use an old cliché, many are called to the author ranks, but a lot fewer seem to be chosen. Some authors who were sure they would "go places" in their careers found only dead ends, partial or low degrees of success, or frustration at not being able to write the specific kind of book that haunts them. On the other hand, dedication, motivation, and determination, applied long enough and in the right way, can bring rewarding results.

There is an unknown factor that leads to great success in writing as well as in any other field. One author of this book calls it X-plus. X-plus is that something extra deep within a person that drives him or her to get ahead. X-plus makes a person move out in front and go to the top of his or her profession or vocation. Some call it "that certain something," while others label it as simply ambition.

Whatever X-plus is, the person who has it (author or not), or eventually develops it, knows it. Grisham has it; Clancy too. Clive

Cussler certainly has it; as does Barbara Taylor Bradford and Mary Higgins Clark. A great example of an author who was loaded with X-plus was Isaac Asimov, who left an astonishing total of over four hundred published books with many of them bestsellers.

The decision to spend your life as an author also implies, and certainly involves, being willing to keep up with the ongoing changes in the industry. Authors can no longer isolate themselves in their ivory towers, only emerging when they have finished work. They must wear many hats today, including those of promoter, salesperson, tour organizer, publicity seeker, speaker, possible panelist, and tracer (of editors, publishers, rights people, book reviewers, columnists, and bookstore owners and managers). The author's career and work now mean being and functioning as a glorified public relations person (or executive, if you wish to think of it that way).

Doctors and lawyers and other professionals must update their knowledge and keep fresh with new information that comes out daily. Why not authors, too? A case in point is the industry news that Germany's giant media conglomerate Bertelsmann recently bought Random House. Overnight, American trade publishing was changed by the move.

Random House remains the nation's largest trade publisher, but with its merger into Bertelsmann, the combined revenues now total about $1.8 billion as of 1998. Before its acquisition, Bertelsmann was the country's fourth largest publisher with total revenues of approximately $650 million.

Knowing who has bought what company, who has merged with one or more other companies, and who owns who in general can affect an author's decision whether or not to communicate with certain publishers. Keeping tabs on the trends and changes in a publisher's list, and other factors that are potentially important, is every writer's responsibility. We are relunctant to provide examples here since the way changes are happening in the industry, they could easily be outdated within weeks or months.

If authorship is your true calling, and if you are determined to devote your life to it, or if you are already doing so as an experienced professional with one or more books to your credit (or twenty), the authors of this book wish you well and Godspeed. Whatever the sacrifice, hardships, or problems you face (or endure now) as you build your career, each time you hold a new book in your hands, knowing that you brought it into the world, deep in your heart and spirit you will know it was worth it.

May your books make their way smoothly into the marketplace; entertain, inform, fascinate many readers, perhaps even change their lives for the better; and soar to the heights of success as your special children doing you proud, enriching lives, and in each of their ways making the world a better place. More author power to you.

APPENDIX   A

—◆—

Questions and Answers
to Guide You

Many people have attended parties or dinners on Friday evenings
and announced to friends or other guests, during conversations, that
they're going to write a book starting on Monday. Sadly, something
short-circuits their resolve when Monday rolls around. Who knows?
Perhaps all they needed was some encouragement and a willingness to
make the commitment to actually complete a book.

This section provides the answers to some of the most frequently
asked questions about writing and selling books. They were selected
from conferences, conventions, and seminars for writers and would-
be authors.

Q. Does a first novel have a chance of being published?
A. Absolutely. Despite the overpublished world we live in, first-time
    novelists are breaking into the marketplace and seeing their books
    do well and even become bestsellers. It depends of course on the
    book and if it gets the right breaks. Rafael Yglesias was acclaimed

183

for his first novel at the amazing age of sixteen. His first two books, *Hide Fox* and *All After*, were published in 1968. His latest book traces the life of a psychiatrist from childhood and is titled *Dr. Neruda's Cure for Evil.*

Another determined author, Frank Baldwin, quit a day job and delivered pizzas for a year while completing *Balling the Jack*, a humorous story set in New York.

Q. Who owns the copyright on a book, the author or publisher?

A. Most publishers are willing to take out the copyright in the author's name, assuming the author asks that it be done this way. The author must request it in some cases. Most agents will take care of this automatically.

Regardless of how it is handled, the author of the work owns the copyright and assigns certain rights to the publisher to control on the author's behalf.

Q. When an author sells a first novel or nonfiction book, is it better to stick with that same publisher on future books or move on to other companies?

A. Many publishers used to include a clause in their contracts giving them an option on an author's next book. Some companies now omit this clause. If an author is happy with a particular publisher, and likes the way his or her book was done, that relationship could lead to other books.

Q. How much money can be made writing books?

A. Anywhere from a few thousand dollars to multimillions. A lot depends on the book, if it takes off in sales, gets the promotion sometimes necessary, and the right timing. Word-of-mouth advertising can help greatly as well as author appearances on *Today*, *Oprah Winfrey*, *Good Morning America*, and other talk shows.

Q. Are "inside contacts" necessary to sell a book?

A. They might improve your chances, but the right book at the right time with the right editor behind it can work wonders. Authors need to be persistent, and this includes veteran pros with impressive track records as well as newcomers working on their first books.

Q. Would it be a mistake to try a romance novel given the glut of such books in the stores?

A. According to the Romance Writers of America, this genre churns out a whopping $1 billion a year. As you know, there is a lot of competition in this field, and established romance authors, mostly women (Nora Roberts, Joann Ross), have devoted fans eager to buy and read their new books. It's worth trying to carve your own place in this genre if romance fiction seems to be calling you.

Q. Do good or bad reviews help or hurt sales of a book?

A. Good reviews can increase sales, but negative ones do not usually determine a book's destiny. Many in the industry think reviews don't have much effect. Any kind of review, good or not so good, is better than none.

Q. Which book publisher is the largest?

A. Random House is still the largest trade publisher in the English-speaking world, despite its purchase by a huge conglomerate.

Q. Can two or more books be written at the same time?

A. Some authors are able to juggle several books at the same time. For most of us, however, one at a time is probably the better part of wisdom. If you try to write two or more novels at the same time, for example, you better have an ingenious memory.

Isaac Asimov could do a book in a week or two, and some authors have tried additional works at the same time, but each individual book deserves an author's full focus.

Q. Which publisher has had the most bestsellers?

A. Over the years it has been Doubleday. One reference source lists Doubleday way up in front, but this could easily change.

Q. Do publishers return rejected material?

A. Some will; some won't. One bestselling author recently received a letter of interest from Pocket Books and a request to see a proposal. (Pocket is a mass-market paperback company.) Three months later, the author got an unsigned, rude letter stating that Pocket Books does not have to return material.

The bottom line is this: An author needs an agent with power in order to deal with some of the mass-market publishers. Pocket Books would not have dared to treat a strong agent the way the author was ill-treated.

Publishers in other sections of the nation, and also in countries overseas, will usually return rejected material they originally asked to see. Some in New York will do so, though the emphasis is on "some." It depends on who the publisher is. Just be aware that if you have no agent, you may never get your proposals and material back. There are no guarantees when dealing with some of these companies unless you're a household name.

Unagented authors communicate at the mercy and whim of certain New York companies. It's a buyer's market, and authors without powerful agents behind them are sometimes abused. This is the simple truth and shows what a disadvantage any author without an agent faces up front.

One solution is worth remembering. Until you are represented by a powerful (or at least strong) agent, avoid major New York publishers and deal only with smaller, regional publishers who still, on the whole, treat authors with respect and professionalism. This advice will save you abuse, time, effort, worry, and losing material that is not returned.

Q. Which is harder? Finding a publisher or finding an agent?
A. Finding an agent, a quality one with clout, is much harder—especially in today's publishing era. One well-known author recently complained that even with his track record of forty published books (no shabby record), he can't find an agent. It's a bit incredible.

Q. How does an author ever land an agent if that is the case?
A. You settle for a lesser known, less influential, less powerful agent, perhaps outside New York, and forget the powerhouse Manhattan agents mainly seeking the à la Grisham, Clancy, megamillion-dollar

author who already has a big name. Some of these power-crazed agents are unbelievable prima donnas who enjoy stepping on unagented authors and abusing them. Don't waste your time and efforts contacting them. Seek out the new, smaller agent who is far more likely to treat you with courtesy and respect, whether they like your book projects or not. Look for these smaller agents outside New York mostly.

Q. Is it true that if one can write a book, one could also possibly write a television script, screenplay, magazine articles, or newspaper column?

A. It's generally true, but a lot depends on the particular writer. Some have at least the potential talent to write almost anything. Others prefer to specialize. A real writer, however, should be able to do almost any type of work with some study and revision.

Dealing with Hollywood and the film colony can be even stranger and more difficult than dealing with the New York publishing arena. L. P. Wilbur had some correspondence with Rod Serling, creator and writer of *The Twilight Zone*. He made a big name for himself in television but eventually realized some years before his death that he preferred to do books. As Rod put it: "I will never work in TV again. It's too tough to be creative, to be unfettered in TV. TV was good to me, but I'm never going back. Oh, how I love the ease and freedom of writing books." One wonders if some of the rude, prima donna New York agents would have accepted Rod as a client!

Q. Doesn't it usually take years of loneliness and struggle to develop a really fine book idea into a strong manuscript?

A. Most fine books take time, but there are exceptions. Some books are so well done that word-of-mouth advertising takes over and can reduce the time. Authors who cannot stop rewriting, however, can take decades on a single book, but they are few in number.

Q. Do publishers get angry or irritated if a book is offered to them on auction (submitted to a number of publishers for the best offer)?

A. Agents do it when they believe the book justifies it, but some publishers don't like it when an author attempts to auction a property.

Publishers generally feel the book being auctioned must be worth it, be a commercial and important subject. They also expect the rules for any auction to be spelled out—i.e., a deadline date for responding with an offer must be specified. The auctioneer often sets a "floor price," which is the minimum that will be accepted.

Q. Which is best to work with? A small, medium, or large book publisher?

A. You should try all three and then go with your gut feeling and the publisher you have the best rapport with or who seems to be most enthusiastic about working with you.

Keep in mind that some small publishers may be able to give your book more attention than large publishers. The larger companies usually offer the better advances, which can be helpful while you are working on the manuscript. Once you have had a book published by all three of these sized publishers, you will know which is best for you. Most authors don't care about size and are just pleased to find a publisher for their work.

Q. Should an author write about only what he or she knows?

A. This question keeps popping up. An author should feel free to write on any subject under the sun that is of interest to him or her. Some publishers miss out on good books because they insist that certain subjects be done by experts only. For medical books, perhaps that is best, but not for all other books.

Let's face it. Most authors would run out of material fast if they had to be experts on each subject they chose. In effect, they become experts from the research and interviews they do for their books. Nonfiction comes to mind here mostly.

Q. Don't most authors need a sympathetic editor?

A. Many do, and this is a key reason why a lot of authors prefer to work with an editor who has done some writing.

Q. What is the most important element needed for writing a bestseller?

A. Luck—many would say timing. In the case of novels, a riveting idea is a must with the enormous competition of today. For non-fiction, the right subject and right time are very crucial. Sometimes a nonfiction book comes along that hits at the start of a trend. Sometimes the book even triggers the trend. Such a book could skyrocket in sales and demand.

Q. Won't the many publishing mergers and buyouts continually going on in the industry mean a tougher time for unknown or lesser-known authors?

A. Yes, to a degree, but there will always be publishers, large and small, who will recognize the value of good books and publish them, whether the author is well known or a newcomer.

Q. Isn't the space problem in most bookstores getting worse?

A. Most definitely, and it's one of the major problems today. This is why the focus is on publishing books that will move off the shelves and into the hands of customers.

   The shelf life of new books is incredibly short unless it starts to move. If a new book does not sell quickly, it is returned to the publisher to make room for the new ones that are constantly arriving.

Q. Must an advance against royalties on a book be paid back by an author if the book does not sell?

A. Some publishers used to include a contract clause stating that unearned advances had to be paid back. Now an author is usually allowed to keep the advance. There are still a few publishers around who may require the advance to be paid back if enough copies don't sell to cover it.

Reference Nuggets to Nourish You

- Once you find a publisher or agent who treats you fairly and professionally, stick with them.

- The query letter, whether sent via e-mail, fax, or snail mail, gives you psychological insurance. Do not send material to a publisher without permission. Always make contact first to see if there is any interest.

- Many books seek only to entertain the reader and often become bestsellers because they do it well.

- The first book an author does is often the most difficult. It gets a bit easier after the first. Obviously, some books can be painful or quite hard to write.

- Remember that, as an author, you can go almost anywhere. All you need are paper, pens, word processor, computer, laptop, fax machine, or whatever. Authors are some of the freest people in the world.

- The staple of many publishers is the trade book. Backlist titles that bring in money year after year do much to keep publishing companies functioning.

- In most cases, an outline will make it easier to write a nonfiction book. A synopsis can also help a lot if your book is a novel.

- "Clear writing is clear thinking." Many a good book has been written on this basic premise.

- Enough research lets you know if an idea is really a good one or one you want to develop.

- One alert author traveled some 16,000 miles all over the country to visit amusement parks. She was gathering material for a nonfiction book about merry-go-rounds.

- It is a must to check the search engines found on most online bookstores, as well as *Books in Print* to see what other books have been published on a subject that interests you.

- Deadlines in a book contract help an author to finish a project. Most book contracts state when a manuscript is to be delivered to the publisher.

- Word-of-mouth advertising is some of the best and can help a book to sell big time, but anything an author can do for his or her book will help.

- One major book club paid five figures for a nonfiction title on knitting. Try to pick timeless subjects that will be continuous sellers.

- Books picked by Oprah's Book Club are selling over a million copies.

Writer's Resources

Suggested Reading

How to Write and Sell Your First Novel (Writers Digest Books)
by Oscar Collier and Frances Spatz Leighton

Writing for Interactive Media: The Complete Guide (Allworth Press)
by Jon Samsel and Darryl Wimberley

How to Write Articles That Sell (Allworth Press)
by L. Perry Wilbur and Jon Samsel

The Writer's Resource Handbook (Allworth Press)
by Daniel Grant

The Writer's Guide to Corporate Communications (Allworth Press)
by Mary Moreno

Business and Legal Forms for Authors and Self-Publishers (Allworth Press)
by Tad Crawford

The Writer's Legal Guide (Allworth Press)
by Tad Crawford and Tony Lyons

Mastering the Business of Writing (Allworth Press)
by Richard Curtis

How to Write and Sell Your First Nonfiction Book (St. Martin's Press)
by Oscar Collier and Frances Spatz Leighton

How to Write What You Want and Sell What You Write: A Complete Guide to Writing and Selling Everything from Ads to Zingers (Career Press)
by Skip Press

How to Write a Book Proposal (Writers Digest Books)
by Michael Larsen

Writer's Guide to Book Editors, Publishers, and Literary Agents (Prima Publishing)
by Jeff Herman

The Awful Truth about Publishing (Warner Books)
by John Boswell

Beyond the Bestseller (New American Library)
by Richard Curtis

Aspects of the Novel (Harcourt Brace Jovanovich)
by E. M. Forster

Writing Resources on the Web

- Publishers Marketing Association (*www.pma-online.org*)
- For Writers Only (*www.webwitch.com/writers*)
- Dial-a-Book (*www.psi.net/dialabook*)
- Writing Resources (*www.teleport.com/~cdeemer/General.html*)
- Inkspot: The Writer's Resource (*www.inkspot.com*)
- Publisher's Catalogs Home Page (*www.lights.com/publisher*)

Writing Conferences

Writer's Roundtable Conference
Conference Director: Deborah Morris
P.O. Box 461572
Garland, TX 75046-1572
Tel. (800) 473-2538, ext. 5
Media contacts: (972) 495-7388, ext. 2
E-mail: *director@wrc-online.com*

The Bread Loaf Writers' Conference
Correspondence: Mrs. Carol Knauss
Middlebury College
Middlebury, VT 05753
Tel. (802) 443-5286
E-mail: *BLWC@mail.middlebury.edu*

Heartland Writers Conference
2683 South Big Bend Boulevard
St. Louis, MO 63143
Tel. (573) 297-3352
E-mail: *hwg@mailexcite.com*

Maui Writers Conference (Labor Day Weekend)
P.O. Box 1118
Kihei, HI 96753
Tel. (808) 879-0061
E-mail: *writers@maui.net*

Mendocino Coast Writers Conference
MCWC Conference Chair: Suzanne Byerley
College of the Redwoods
1211 Del Mar Drive
Fort Bragg, CA 95437
Tel. (707) 961-1001
E-mail: *mcwrite@mail.redwoods.cc.ca.us*

Southern California Writer's Conference
2596 Escondido Avenue
San Diego, CA 92123
Tel. (619) 291-6805
E-mail: *scwcsd@aol.com*

Willamette Writers Conference
9045 SW Barbur Boulevard, Suite 5A
Portland, OR 97219
E-mail: *wilwrite@teleport.com*

Magazines and Journals

ByLine
P.O. Box 130596
Edmond, OK 73013
    Monthly national magazine aimed toward helping writers succeed.
Includes articles on the craft or business of writing. Publishes short
fiction and poetry, with a special feature for student writers. Sponsors
monthly writing contests with cash prizes.

Children's Book Insider
P.O. Box 1030
Fort Collins, CO 80440-1030
Tel. (719) 836-0394.
Web site: *www.write4kids.com*
    Monthly publication with useful market information for those writ-
ing for children, as well as how-to articles. You can get more informa-
tion by visiting the Children's Writing Resource Center on the Web.

Children's Writer
95 Long Ridge Road
West Redding, CT 06896
Tel. (800) 443-6078
    Monthly newsletter published by the Institute of Children's
Literature. It includes how-to stories, author interviews, and market
updates with editors' names.

New Writer's Newsletter
Dept.-S, 4202 Fairway
Pasadena, TX 77505
   Specifically aimed at helping new writers get published, but published writers will also find plenty to interest them.

Once Upon A Time . . .
553 Winston Court
St. Paul, MN 55118
E-mail: *AudreyOUAT@aol.com*
   Issued every three months, this thirty-two-page magazine for children's authors and illustrators describes itself as "a substitute for the backyard fence." The magazine also has a Web site at: *http://members.aol.com/OUATMAG*.

Publishers Weekly
249 West 17th Street
New York, NY, 10011
Tel. (800) 278-2991
   Expensive weekly magazine for industry professionals. Includes detailed analyses of market segments, publishing trends, bestseller lists, lists of who is publishing what, author interviews, book reviews, and a weekly section on the juvenile market. Available in most public libraries.

SCBWI Bulletin
22736 Vanowen Street, Suite 106
West Hills, CA., 91307
Tel. (818) 888-8760
Web site: *www.scbwi.org/bulletin.htm*
   Bimonthly publication of the Society of Children's Book Writers and Illustrators. Features market updates, interviews, names and news about members, upcoming events of interest to children's writers and illustrators, etc. The *Bulletin* is included with annual membership.

School Library Journal
245 West 17th Street
New York, NY 10011
Tel. (212) 463-6759

   A highly regarded publication for librarians serving children and adolescents in schools and public libraries. Monthly issues include not only news about the field, but also articles and columns dealing with reading issues related to children.

The Writer
120 Boylston Street
Boston, MA 02116-4615

   General information magazine for writers of all genres. Included are market updates, interviews with authors, and advice columns.

Writer's Digest
P.O. Box 2124
Harlan, IA 51593-2313

   The most widely read writer's magazine in circulation.

Index

Books from Allworth Press

Writing for Interactive Media: The Complete Guide by Jon Samsel and Darryl Wimberley (hardcover, 6 × 9, 320 pages, $19.95)

How to Write Articles That Sell, Second Edition by L. Perry Wilbur and Jon Samsel (hardcover, 6 × 9, 224 pages, $19.95)

The Writer's and Photographer's Guide to Global Markets by Michael Sedge (hardcover, 6 × 9, 288 pages, $19.95)

The Writer's Legal Guide, Revised Edition by Tad Crawford and Tony Lyons (hardcover, 6 × 9, 320 pages, $19.95)

This Business of Publishing: An Insider's View of Current Trends and Tactics by Richard Curtis (softcover, 6 × 9, 224 pages, $18.95)

The Writer's Resource Handbook by Daniel Grant (softcover, 6 × 9, 272 pages, $19.95)

The Writer's Internet Handbook by Timothy K. Maloy (softcover, 6 × 9, 192 pages, $18.95)

Business and Legal Forms for Authors and Self-Publishers, Revised Edition by Tad Crawford (softcover, 8½ × 11, 192 pages, $19.95)

Mastering the Business of Writing: A Leading Literary Agent Reveals the Secrets of Success by Richard Curtis (softcover, 6 × 9, 272 pages, $18.95)

Photography for Writers: Using Photography to Increase Your Writing Income by Michael Havelin (softcover, 6 × 9, 224 pages, $18.95)

The Writer's Guide to Corporate Communications by Mary Moreno (softcover, 6 × 9, 192 pages, $18.95)

The Internet Publicity Guide: How to Maximize Your Marketing and Promotion in Cyberspace by V. A. Shiva (softcover, 6 × 9, 224 pages, $18.95)

The Copyright Guide: A Friendly Guide for Protecting and Profiting from Copyrights by Lee Wilson (softcover, 6 × 9, 192 pages, $18.95)

Please write to request our free catalog. To order by credit card, call 1-800-491-2808 or send a check or money order to Allworth Press, 10 East 23rd Street, Suite 210, New York, NY 10010. Include $5 for shipping and handling for the first book ordered and $1 for each additional book. Ten dollars plus $1 for each additional book if ordering from Canada. New York State residents must add sales tax.

If you would like to see our complete catalog on the World Wide Web, you can find us at *www.allworth.com*.